Follow Stone Church Brook by walking on the flat rocks.

HIKING NEW YORK'S LOWER HUDSON VALLEY

Randi Minetor
Photographs by Nic Minetor

FALCONGUIDES

GUILFORD, CONNECTICUT

FALCONGUIDES®

An imprint of Globe Pequot

Falcon and FalconGuides are registered trademarks and Make Adventure Your Story is a trademark of Rowman & Littlefield.

Distributed by NATIONAL BOOK NETWORK
Copyright © 2018 by Rowman & Littlefield
Photos by Nic Minetor unless otherwise noted.
TOPO! Maps copyright © 2018 National Geographic Partners, LLC. All Rights Reserved.
Maps: © Rowman & Littlefield

British Library Cataloguing in Publication Information available

Library of Congress Cataloging-in-Publication Data

Names: Minetor, Randi, author.
Title: Hiking New York's lower Hudson Valley / Randi Minetor ; photographs by
  Nic Minetor.
Description: Guilford, Connecticut : FalconGuides, 2018. | Includes index. |
  Identifiers: LCCN 2017059212 (print) | LCCN 2017060657 (ebook) | ISBN |
  ISBN 9781493029891 (pbk.) | ISBN 9781493029907 (e-book)
Subjects: LCSH: Hiking—Hudson River Valley (N.Y. and N.J.)—Guidebooks. |
  Trails—Hudson River Valley (N.Y. and N.J.)—Guidebooks. | Hudson River
  Valley (N.Y. and N.J.)—Guidebooks.
Classification: LCC GV199.42.H83 (ebook) | LCC GV199.42.H83 M56 2018 (print)
  | DDC 796.5109747/3—dc23
LC record available at https://lccn.loc.gov/2017059212

∞™ The paper used in this publication meets the minimum requirements of American National Standard for Information Sciences—Permanence of Paper for Printed Library Materials, ANSI/NISO Z39.48-1992.

Printed in the United States of America

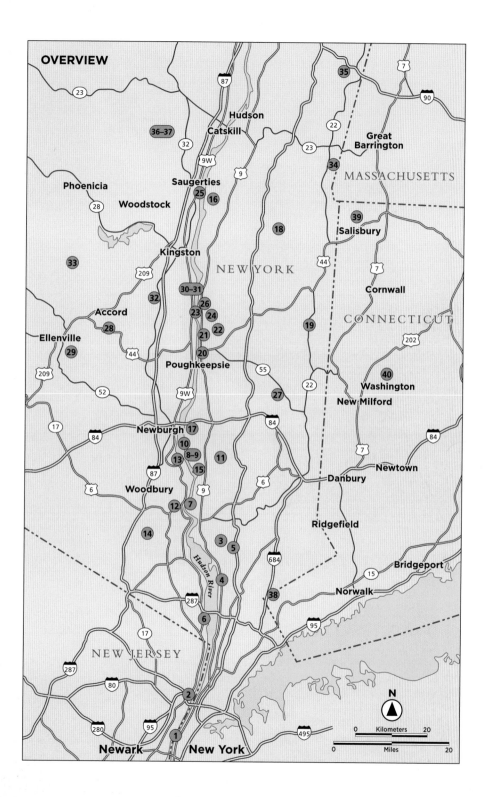

The short, steep hike is more than worth the effort to see the magnificent Kaaterskill Falls.

THE HIKES

ACKNOWLEDGMENTS	viii
MEET YOUR GUIDES	x
MAP AND ICON LEGENDS	xi
TRAIL FINDER	xii
TOP FIVE HIKES	xiv
BEFORE YOU HIT THE TRAIL	1
HUDSON VALLEY OVERVIEW	1
WEATHER	4
FLORA AND FAUNA	5
WILDERNESS REGULATIONS	10

THE HIKES

New York City and the Palisades

1. High Line Park	15
2. Fort Lee Historic Park: Shore Trail–Long Path Loop	20
3. Croton Gorge Park	27
4. Old Croton Aqueduct Trail: Scarborough to Sleepy Hollow	33
5. Teatown Lake Reservation	39
6. Piermont Marsh and Pier	44
7. Anthony's Nose	49

Putnam and Orange Counties

8. Little Stony Point	56
9. Hudson Highlands State Park Preserve: Cornish Estate–Undercliff Trail Loop	62
10. Breakneck Ridge	69
11. Clarence Fahnestock Memorial State Park: Three Lakes Trail	74
12. Bear Mountain State Park: Appalachian Trail to the Summit	80

13. Storm King Mountain and Butter Hill   85
14. Harriman State Park: Pine Swamp Mountain   91
15. Constitution Marsh Audubon Center and Sanctuary   97

Dutchess County

16. Tivoli Bays Wildlife Management Area   104
17. Mount Beacon Park   109
18. Thompson Pond   114
19. Dover Stone Church   120
20. Locust Grove   125
21. Walkway Over the Hudson State Historic Park and
    Loop Trail   130
22. Peach Hill Park   135
23. Hyde Park Trail: Roosevelt and Vanderbilt National
    Historic Sites   140
24. Top Cottage and Eleanor Roosevelt Estate   148
25. Falling Waters Preserve   153
26. Winnakee Nature Preserve   159
27. Mount Egbert via the Appalachian Trail   164

Ulster County

28. Minnewaska State Park Preserve: Minnewaska Lake
    Carriage Road   171
29. Minnewaska State Park Preserve, Sam's Point Area:
    Loop Road to the Ice Caves   176
30. Black Creek Preserve   181
31. Shaupeneak Ridge: Ridge Trail   187
32. Wallkill Valley Rail Trail: New Paltz to Rosendale   192
33. Upper Vernooy Kill Falls Trail   198

Columbia and Greene Counties

34. Taconic State Park: Copake Falls Mine Area and
    Bash Bish Falls   205
35. Beebe Hill Fire Tower   210
36. North-South Lake Park: Catskill Escarpment Loop   216
37. Kaaterskill and Bastion Falls   222

Western Connecticut

38. The Audubon Center in Greenwich   228
39. Lion's Head   234
40. Steep Rock Preserve: Steep Rock Loop   239

BONUS HIKES   244
LOCAL INTEREST TRAIL FINDER   253
INDEX   255
ABOUT THE AUTHOR AND PHOTOGRAPHER   256

ACKNOWLEDGMENTS

I have been blessed over the past eleven years with a wonderful partnership with the folks at FalconGuides, for whom I have written more than twenty books. I thank my editor, Evan Helmlinger, for offering Nic and me the opportunity to return to the Hudson River Valley and get to know it more intimately than ever before. I also must acknowledge the terrific work that the editing and production staff does to make Falcon's hiking and nature guides such excellent resources in the field. It's been a heck of a ride, and I know there will be more to come.

Many people have helped make certain that the information provided in these trail descriptions is accurate and up to date. I wish to thank McCrea Burnham of the New York State Department of Environmental Conservation; Linda Cooper and Evan Thompson of the New York State Office of Parks, Recreation, and Historic Preservation; Eric Nelsen and Matthew Shook of the Palisades Interstate Park Commission; Karl Beard of the National Park Service; Curtis Rand of the Salisbury Parks and Forest Commission; Reed Sparling and Rita Shaheen of Scenic Hudson; Lori Paradis Brant of the Steep Rock Association; Leigh Draper at Teatown Lake Reservation; Ted Gilman at the Audubon Center at Greenwich; Katie House of the Town of Dover; Tom Weyering at the Town of Poughkeepsie; Paul Gallery at The Nature Conservancy; Jorge Gomes at Minnewaska State Park Preserve; Michael Reade at the Wallkill Valley Rail Trail Association; Gregg H. Swanzey of the Winnakee Land Trust; Cub Barrett at Friends of the High Line; Eric Lind at Constitution Marsh Audubon Center; and Kenneth Snodgrass at Locust Grove. Each of these people carefully reviewed the material in a timely manner, helping me bring you a stronger guide.

In selecting the hikes for this book, I tapped into some extraordinary resources already available online. In particular, I tip my Tilley hat to the New York–New Jersey Trail Conference for their extraordinary maps, without which I might still be lost and confused in the wilderness. I am especially grateful to Mike Todd of HikeTheHudsonValley.com, both for the great guidance his website provided during our trail selection process and for helping out when I found Breakneck Ridge to be more than I could handle.

No book I write would be complete without expressing my gratitude to my dear friends who support every project Nic and I undertake, no matter how bizarre or far-reaching some of these turn out to be. Ken Horowitz and Rose-Anne Moore, Martha and Peter Schermerhorn, Ruth Watson and John King, and a band of merry Renegade Writers including Sandra Beckwith, Tori DeAngelis, Rachel Dickinson, Stacey Freed, Mark Obbie, Aline Alexander Newman, and Gina Roberts-Gray provide the unconditional positive regard that keeps me at the keyboard.

And to all the people who build and maintain trails throughout the lower Hudson Valley, I can hardly begin to express my gratitude for your dedication to creating high-quality hiking experiences for all. It is my privilege to present the fruits of your labors to readers of this book.

MEET YOUR GUIDES

What a pleasure it was to return to the Hudson River Valley for my fifth book that includes hikes in this area. It's been seven years since *Best Easy Day Hikes: Hudson River Valley* was published, and since then my husband, photographer Nic Minetor, and I have returned to the area while working on *Hiking Waterfalls in New York, Day Trips in the Hudson Valley*, and *Hiking Through History New York*.

Randi Minetor   **Nic Minetor**

I've loved hiking since I was a Girl Scout back in the 1960s—and now, at age 59, I know that hiking is a key factor in staying healthy. Still, I had to be judicious in choosing the hikes in this book, as some health issues keep me from hiking at higher elevations or scrambling up big rock faces. I can say with certainty that if I can complete the hikes in this book (and I did in all but one case), you can too. You'll find plenty to challenge you in these pages, but you'll also discover some fairly easy hikes that may not have come to your attention before.

FIVE HIKING TIPS

Hiking in the Hudson Valley has a special set of challenges. Here are my tips for staying safe, healthy, and upright on the valley's trails.

1. **Carry a stick.** You'll find it much easier to make your way up and down rock-strewn trails if you use a walking stick or ski poles.

2. **Dress against ticks.** Ticks that carry Lyme disease are a serious infestation in this area. Long sleeves, long pants, and plenty of insect repellent will help keep you safe.

3. **Remember to eat.** You may not feel hungry, but when you lose energy half-way up a steep trail, a handy granola bar will restore your drive.

4. **Use a compass.** Electronic devices can tell you which way is north, but there's no cellular or wireless service on many of these trails. Learn to orient yourself with an actual compass. If you've never used one, get out on an easy trail and practice before you take on something harder.

5. **Pack it out.** Don't join others in spoiling the Hudson Valley wilderness. Take your trash with you—and if you can, pick up after others.

Map and Icon Legends

ICON LEGEND

BEST PHOTOS

FAMILY FRIENDLY

WATER FEATURES

DOG FRIENDLY

FINDING SOLITUDE

NOTES ON MAPS

Topographic maps are essential companions to the activities in this guide. Falcon has partnered with National Geographic to provide the best mapping resources. Each activity is accompanied by a detailed map and the name of the National Geographic TOPO! map (USGS), which can be downloaded for free from natgeomaps.com.

If the activity takes place on a National Geographic Trails Illustrated map, it will be noted. Continually setting the standard for accuracy, each Trails Illustrated topographic map is crafted in conjunction with local land managers and undergoes rigorous review and enhancement before being printed on waterproof, tear-resistant material. Trails Illustrated maps and information about their digital versions, which can be used on mobile GPS applications, can be found at natgeomaps.com.

MAP LEGEND

87 Interstate	**Gate**
9W US Highway	**Park**
9 State Highway	**P** Parking
County/Forest/Local Road	**Picnic Area**
Unpaved Road	**Point of Interest**
Railroad	**Restroom**
Featured Route on Trail	**Shelter**
Trail	**1** Trailhead
Stairs or Boardwalk	**Viewpoint**
Bench	**?** Visitor Center
Bridge	**Waterfall**
Cave	

	BEST PHOTOS	FAMILY FRIENDLY	WATER FEATURES	DOG FRIENDLY	FINDING SOLITUDE
1. High Line		•			
2. Fort Lee Historic Park: Shore Trail–Long Path Loop		•			
3. Croton Gorge Park		•	•	•	
4. Old Croton Aqueduct		•			
5. Teatown Lake Reservation		•		•	
6. Piermont Marsh and Pier		•	•		
7. Anthony's Nose	•				
8. Little Stony Point		•	•	•	
9. Hudson Highlands State Park Preserve: Cornish Estate–Undercliff Trail Loop	•			•	
10. Breakneck Ridge	•				
11. Clarence Fahnestock Memorial State Park: Three Lakes Trail				•	•
12. Bear Mountain State Park: Appalachian Trail to the Summit	•			•	
13. Storm King Mountain and Butter Hill	•				
14. Harriman State Park: Pine Swamp Mountain	•			•	•
15. Constitution Marsh Audubon Center and Sanctuary		•	•		
16. Tivoli Bays WMA		•	•	•	
17. Mount Beacon Park	•			•	
18. Thompson Pond		•	•		
19. Dover Stone Church		•	•	•	
20. Locust Grove		•		•	
21. Walkway Over the Hudson State Historical Park		•	•	•	

	BEST PHOTOS	FAMILY FRIENDLY	WATER FEATURES	DOG FRIENDLY	FINDING SOLITUDE
22. Peach Hill Park				•	•
23. Hyde Park Trail: Roosevelt and Vanderbilt National Historic Sites		•	•	•	
24. Top Cottage and Eleanor Roosevelt Estates					•
25. Falling Waters Preserve			•	•	•
26. Winnakee Nature Preserve		•		•	
27. Mount Egbert via the AT				•	•
28. Minnewaska Lake Carriage Road		•	•		
29. Minnewaska: Ice Caves		•			
30. Black Creek Preserve		•	•		
31. Shaupeneak Ridge: Ridge Trail	•				•
32. Wallkill Valley Rail Trail	•	•			
33. Upper Vernooy Kill Falls Trail			•		
34. Taconic State Park: Copake Falls Mine Area and Bash Bish Falls		•	•		
35. Beebe Hill Fire Tower					•
36. North-South Lake Park: Catskill Escarpment Loop	•		•		
37. Kaaterskill and Bastion Falls	•		•		
38. The Audubon Center in Greenwich		•			
39. Lion's Head	•				
40. Steep Rock Preserve: Steep Rock Loop	•				

BEAR MOUNTAIN: It's not the highest mountain in the area, but Bear may be the most beloved for the magnificent vistas at multiple viewpoints. Recent Appalachian Trail work makes this an especially satisfying hike.

BEAR MOUNTAIN

CLARENCE FAHNESTOCK
MEMORIAL STATE PARK
THREE LAKES TRAIL

CLARENCE FAHNESTOCK MEMORIAL STATE PARK THREE LAKES TRAIL: It's tough to find solitude in the Hudson Valley, but this trail leads directly to it—with the pleasures of well-marked trails, open lakes, beaver activity, marshes, stream crossings, and a particularly lovely forest.

MOUNT BEACON: A solid combination of heart-pumping switchbacks and sweeping views, this hike delivers both a physical challenge and a spectacular visual payoff.

MOUNT BEACON

NORTH-SOUTH LAKE PARK CATSKILL ESCARPMENT LOOP WITH THE KAATERSKILL FALLS SPUR: There's no better place to experience the vast green wilderness that is the Catskill Mountains, with the bonus of a top view of the state's highest waterfall.

NORTH-SOUTH LAKE
PARK CATSKILL
ESCARPMENT LOOP

CONSTITUTION MARSH AUDUBON CENTER: Beautifully maintained with a boardwalk that extends well into the marsh, this bird lover's paradise offers expansive water views.

CONSTITUTION MARSH
AUDUBON CENTER

HUDSON VALLEY OVERVIEW

If you've driven your car or taken the Metro-North line through the rolling green mountains of the Hudson River Valley and wondered what more might lie beyond the windows of your vehicle, here is your chance to discover this region's hidden places and scenic wonders.

Stand atop Mount Beacon or Breakneck Ridge in the Hudson Highlands and see the glory of the river—a mile-wide glistening ribbon curving through the valley, lined with woodland-covered hills and mountains for miles in either direction. Here stand the uniformly emerald deciduous forests of red maple, oak, beech, and birch, relieving eyes fatigued by cityscapes and filling lungs with fresh oxygen. Here also rise mountains of a manageable height—(mostly) less than 2,000 feet—allowing morning hikers to reach a summit and enjoy the reward of an expansive view by lunchtime.

This wealth of accessible natural surroundings, much of it just a train station away from New York City, has made the Hudson Valley an immensely popular place in recent years. Park rangers will tell you that an explosion of interest in trails in Hudson Highlands, Bear Mountain, Harriman, High Tor, Hook Mountain, and Storm King State

Fall in the Hudson Valley offers brilliant color and beautiful views.

Get up close to the Hudson River shore in Palisades Interstate Park.

Parks has created a steady stream of weekend hikers on most trails throughout spring, summer, and fall. Beyond the parks that can be reached by train, Minnewaska State Park Preserve, Mohonk Preserve, Shawangunk Ridge, and others in Catskill Park have had to examine overflow parking options for the glut of explorers who come to hike the trails on weekends.

Don't let the prospect of other hikers on the trails discourage you, however; these parks have enough trail options to accommodate everyone. The trails detailed in this book are just a sample of the amazing places you can wander as you discover the pleasures of hiking in the Hudson Valley.

Considering that this wealth of open landscape exists just down the road from the largest city (by population) in the United States, what kept all this land from becoming a network of housing tracts and condominiums? Indeed, over the last two centuries, this land survived attacks from one source after another. The lumber industry stripped these hills bare, allowing silt to slide down into the river and virtually destroying its natural ability to regulate its own water levels. At the south end of the river, railroads blasted through high cliffs to construct the tracks that still bring passengers and cargo through the valley today. Corporations used the river as their primary dumping ground for sewage and chemicals, further marring the banks and the surrounding landscape.

In the face of all this misuse of the river and its hills and mountains, early movements to save the Hudson Valley began as far back as the late 1800s. Wealthy families bought up the available wilderness and transformed it from denuded forests into state parks and preserves. Early environmentalists began a battle to cleanse the river that extended through the twentieth century, culminating in legislation that triggered the national ecology movement. Today we can enjoy the fruits of their success: verdant second-growth forests, wide views of open spaces from clifftops and mountain peaks, and a shining blue river that connects them all.

This book presents just a sampling of the options for hiking your way through the Lower Hudson Valley. I have chosen these hikes to provide a taste of many parks, preserves, historic sites, and sanctuaries in this region—from the banks of the river in northern New Jersey to the top of the escarpment in the Catskill Mountains. I've included trails in western Connecticut and the Taconic Mountain region as well, as these areas feature some terrific hiking experiences and are just a short car ride away for downstate New Yorkers.

As you walk these trails and discover many options for further adventures, please join me in thanking the people and organizations who have made this area such a joy to

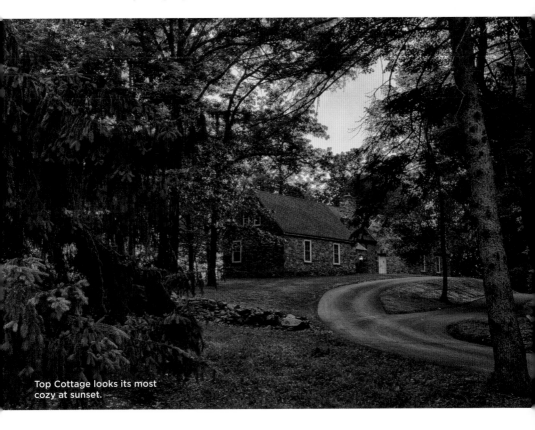

Top Cottage looks its most cozy at sunset.

explore. From the earliest crusaders for preservation to today's trail maintenance crews organized by the Appalachian Mountain Club and the New York–New Jersey Trail Conference, thousands of people have dedicated countless hours to make these paths available to us. We could not be more grateful for this gift of wilderness on the edge of so much bustling civilization.

WEATHER

Few places can match New York State for its gorgeous spring and summer, when flowers scent the air, leaves embrace the trees with intense emerald shades, and the sky turns cobalt to complement the sunlight. The sun shines six days out of ten from June through August, and while spring temperatures can linger in the 50s and 60s until June, idyllic summer days average in the 70s and 80s, with occasional spikes into the 90s in June or July, and cooler temperatures at night. Heavy rains often arrive in April, although they rarely last more than a day or two at a time. The Lower Hudson River Valley has no dry season, so be prepared for rain any time you visit.

Don't miss the hike to the Constitution Marsh boardwalk.

To truly appreciate the transformation to vibrant spring and summer seasons in upstate New York, however, we must face the area's legendary winters. Winter temperatures average in the mid-20s, with significant dips into the teens in January, February, and March. Check the "windchill" before making a winter hike—especially at altitude—as the air can feel much colder than the temperature indicates. The annual late January or early February thaw can push temperatures into the 50s for a few days, but the cold will return, usually lasting on and off into late March. Snow is guaranteed—an average winter has about 63 inches, although not all at once. Check your selected park's website before attempting any winter hike—the trail may be impassable after a heavy snow, or the road to the trailhead may be closed.

The Hudson Valley area enjoys a high percentage of sunny days—as much as 67 percent in summer; nearly 40 percent even in the doldrums of winter. Cloudy days can make for exciting photos from mountain summits or open marshes, however, so don't rule out your hike just because the day is overcast. On any day when sun is likely, be sure to wear sunscreen, especially if you're heading up to a summit or you expect to spend time on an open rock face.

Fall equals spring in its spectacle, with days in the 50s and 60s, bright blue skies, and foliage panoramas all along the river and throughout the area's parks and preserves. The emerald hillsides turn shades of orange, gold, and crimson in fall, making the trails to mountain summits some of the most popular places in the state. If you're planning to hike to see fall foliage, go on a weekday if possible, or hit the trail early in the day. By afternoon, you may have more company than you will enjoy.

FLORA AND FAUNA

The Lower Hudson Valley offers a rich diversity of plant, bird, animal, and insect species, most of which mean you no harm at all. There's something interesting going on just about anywhere you look, and most of what you see requires nothing more than a keen eye and a perceptive ear to identify.

Mountain laurel blooms in June on hills throughout the Hudson Valley.

Forest floors may be carpeted with mayapple and marsh marigold in spring, and then give way to large areas of rattlesnake, evergreen grape, royal, and other ferns. You may see tiny white bunchberry plants growing along forest trails, producing clusters of bright red berries in summer. Tall stalks of yellow and white sweet clover dominate the edges of greenways and rail trails in spring and early summer, while the bright purple and white blooms of dame's rocket overtake fields throughout spring, especially in areas close to water. The flowers of such invasive shrubs as multiflora rose and Tatarian honeysuckle add their intoxicating scent to the clear spring air in forests and along the edges of field trails.

Open meadows become vast expanses of nodding wildflowers in summer, with coneflower, black-eyed Susan, butterfly milkweed, bee balm, common milkweed, blazing star, common fleabane, and joe-pye weed among the most common native blooms. A wide variety of invasive, nonnative flowering plants are mixed in as well, including purple loosestrife, oxeye daisy, garlic mustard, chicory, bindweed, black swallowwort, and several less-aggressive species.

The native tulip tree blooms spectacularly in late May or early June.

Marshes may be filled with tall marsh grasses called phragmites (or common reed), which sport a tassel at the top of a long stalk. Some calm water surfaces host lily pads and white or yellow water lilies; others—including the river surface you can see at Little Stony Point or Falling Waters Preserve—are covered with European water chestnut, an invasive plant that produces the three-cornered pods that you will crunch under your feet as you walk these trails.

Not all plants are friendly. Poison ivy can be found along many trails; keep an eye out for shiny green "leaves of three" and do as the rhyme says: "Let it be." Poison ivy also climbs trees, so before you put out a hand to steady yourself against a tree trunk, look to be sure it isn't wrapped in a suspicious vine. (Virginia creeper also climbs trees and looks similar to poison ivy, but it has five leaves instead of three.)

CRITTERS

You will see many animals as you hike, with gray and red squirrels and eastern chipmunks the most frequent trail companions. White-tailed deer are easy to spot ahead of you on a trail or from a distance as you pass a field. While you will see considerable evidence of beaver activity, especially in Clarence Fahnestock Memorial State Park, you're not likely to see the creatures themselves at work unless you hike early in the morning or close to dusk. Coyotes, red foxes, porcupines, and raccoons are all residents of the region and may put in an appearance.

Black bears, while not common, are a distinct possibility in the Lower Hudson Valley. Nic and I saw bear scat on several trails, and we have spotted bears in the area while working on other books. Take the necessary precautions to avoid startling, or being startled by, a bear:

- **Make noise when hiking.** Bears have only average hearing and rather poor eyesight. Make plenty of noise when you're hiking—talk, sing, call out, and clap your hands at regular intervals. Bear bells generally are not loud enough to let the animals know you're on your way. Once a bear hears you coming, chances are good that he or she will move away from the trail and leave you alone.

- **Assume that bears are nearby.** Even the most popular and well-used trails may go through bear country, so don't assume there are no bears on heavily populated trails. Keep making noise (and ignore the people who give you the evil eye for being noisy), and keep your eyes open for bears in the area.

- **Watch out for surprises.** When you approach streams, shrubs full of berries, fields of cow parsnip, or areas of dense vegetation, keep your eyes open for bears. As they can't always smell or hear you, you may startle a bear by arriving quietly.

- **Do not approach bears.** Bears are not tame, and they are not zoo animals. You have come to their natural habitat in the wild, so steer clear of them as much as possible. Don't try to get closer for a better photo. While deaths from bear attacks have been scant throughout New York's history, hikers in other states and in national parks have been mauled and sustained serious injuries because they tried to get too close—and I've had the dubious honor of writing about a lot of them.

- **Carry bear spray.** Pepper spray is one good defense against a charging bear. Nontoxic and with no permanent effect, it triggers "temporary incapacitating discomfort" in the bear, which can halt an attack and give you the opportunity to get away. If a bear charges you, aim the aerosol directly in the bear's face. This is not a bear repellent—spraying it on yourself (as you would an insect repellent) will not keep bears away.

- **If you encounter a bear, do this.** As every bear will react differently, there is no set protocol that will result in a sure-fire escape. Talk quietly or not at all; the time to make loud noise is before you encounter a bear.

  - Try to detour around the bear if possible.

  - Do not run! Talk calmly so that the bear can tell you're human and therefore not a threat—or prey.

  - Make yourself look larger—move to higher ground if you can. Do not climb a tree. Black bears are good climbers and may follow you.

  - Drop something (not food) to distract the bear. Keep your pack on for protection in case of an attack.

  - If a bear attacks and you have pepper spray, use it!

BUGS AND BUTTERFLIES

Mosquitoes, blackflies, no-see-ums, gnats, and other tiny flying things can make a May or June hike less fun than you intended, so take the necessary precautions. Choose an insect repellent that will ward off the bugs you want to avoid, and use it liberally —it's not cologne or aftershave, it's a protective tool; coat your exposed skin with it. I recommend spraying the inside of your hat brim to help keep bugs off your face and ears.

To escape the more heavily used trails, check out Clarence Fahnestock Memorial State Park.

Deer ticks that carry Lyme disease have become a significant issue in the Lower Hudson Valley. Nic and I hiked all the trails in this book without contracting Lyme disease, so the precautions we took seemed to do the job: We treated all our clothing (especially our socks) with insect repellent made for this purpose, wore additional repellent on any exposed skin, and wore long, lightweight pants and boots that covered our ankles. We also checked carefully after hiking to be sure we hadn't taken on any hitchhiking ticks. The few ticks we saw never made it past our clothing. Lyme disease is a serious illness with potential long-term implications—it may seem like overkill to be so cautious, but it will help keep you from getting sick.

On the positive side, you can look forward to seeing lots of butterflies like yellow swallowtails, black swallowtails, red admirals, monarchs, morning cloaks, and several others. If you love butterflies, plan a hike through an open meadow or a marsh in spring or summer. Tiny green inchworms may dangle in front of you on a single thread of silk on forest trails, working their way to the ground, where they will pupate below the soil and become geometer moths.

BIRDS

More than 300 bird species either pass through the Hudson Valley during spring and fall migration or nest and breed in the area, so you may spot any number of interesting birds, depending on the season. From spring through fall, virtually all the region's forests host red-eyed vireo, wood thrush, veery, yellow warbler, common yellowthroat, ovenbird, gray catbird, house wren, white-breasted nuthatch, American robin, blue jay, northern cardinal, northern flicker, downy and hairy woodpeckers, pileated woodpecker, great-crested flycatcher, chipping sparrow, and other common woodland birds.

A hike that includes open meadows may bring you tree and barn swallows, eastern bluebird, red-winged blackbird, eastern meadowlark, bobolink, savannah sparrow, and northern harrier hunting for small rodents for dinner. Overhead, turkey vultures may circle in their search for carrion; some may glide on the wind at eye level when you reach a mountain summit. Bald eagles are commonly seen dive-fishing along the river.

The ponds and marshy areas are almost sure to attract great blue heron, as well as swamp sparrow, marsh wren, and shorebirds including greater yellowlegs, spotted sandpiper, least and semipalmated sandpipers, and others during their migration. Canada geese are common residents, and many ducks spend spring and summer along the Hudson as well. Keep an eye out for wood duck, hooded merganser, gadwall, American wigeon, and blue-winged and green-winged teal, as well as American coot. Migration may bring northern pintail, common and red-breasted mergansers, greater and lesser scaups, bufflehead, and ruddy duck. Osprey are a common sight along the river, their nests atop utility poles and other very tall structures.

A WORD ABOUT SNAKES

Seventeen snake species occur in New York State, so you may encounter one or two of these as you hike throughout the Hudson Valley region. It's entirely likely that you will spot a completely harmless garter snake or a brown snake on Hudson Valley trails. In some areas, however, it is possible—though uncommon—that you will come across a timber rattlesnake or a copperhead, two of the three venomous snake species that live in this state. (The third, the massasauga rattlesnake, occurs only in two wetlands in central and western New York; it is not found in the Hudson Valley.)

Timber rattlesnakes are a threatened species found primarily in the southeastern portion of New York, though not in New York City. Commercial hunters covet their skins, so these snakes have been pursued into threatened status in recent years, making a sighting a fairly rare occurrence on a downstate trail. Watch for a light-colored snake with large dark brown blotches along its 5- to 6-foot length. You may hear the rattle before you see the snake, although other snakes—threatening and benign—vibrate their tails when they are provoked, making a sound like a rattle when the tail encounters dry leaves.

The Lower Hudson Valley is prime territory for the copperhead, a light brown snake with distinctive bands around its body that widen along its sides. The copperhead's fairly narrow head has a distinctly coppery hue.

If you encounter a venomous snake on a path, keep your distance and let it pass. In most cases, the snake wants as little to do with you as you do with it and will slither away without bothering you—most snakes don't like to attack something too big to eat. If you get too close unexpectedly and the snake does bite, seek medical attention, including antivenin treatment, immediately. The SUNY College of Environmental Science and Forestry (ESF) recommends that you leave snakebite treatment to medical professionals—the kits that suggest that you cut open the wound with a razor blade and suction out the poison are "not recommended" by the ESF. Adults rarely die of these snakebites,

Minnewaska State Park Preserve has one of the most unusual landscapes in New York.

the ESF notes, unless they have a severe allergic reaction to the venom—a very unusual situation.

WILDERNESS REGULATIONS

Most of the hikes in this book cross New York state parks or lands protected by Scenic Hudson, an environmental organization that preserves land and farms and creates parks "that connect people with the inspirational power of the Hudson River," according to its website. Other land protection agencies represented in this book include Audubon, the National Park Service, and local city and county park commissions.

While regulations may differ from one organization to the next—especially where dogs are concerned—they agree on these commonsense rules:

- **Stay within the park boundaries.** Adjacent lands may be privately owned; please be considerate of others' property.

- **Keep dogs leashed, and pick up their waste.** Some properties do not allow dogs; check the listings in this book before you hike.

- **Do not pick flowers, remove plants, or destroy plants or trees.** The adage "Take only memories, leave only footprints" is in effect here.

- **Leave artifacts in place as you found them.** Moving or removing an artifact can diminish its value in revealing facts about the area's history.

- **Carry out all your trash.** This is a rule that many Hudson River Valley hikers neglect to follow, so you will see trash—sometimes piles of it—in some of the most popular areas. Don't consider this permission to leave your own cans and wrappers. Please take your own trash out of the park.

- **Tagging is against the law.** Some popular trails have become graffiti magnets, especially those closer to New York City. Tagging is a Class A misdemeanor in New York State, punishable with fines and up to a year in prison. Resist the urge to follow the example of inconsiderate people who don't understand the value of pristine wilderness.

- **Stay on marked trails.** Using "social trails," like shortcuts across switchbacks, causes hillsides to erode more quickly, which will eventually destroy the landscape. Stick to the nicely cleared, engineered, and maintained trails.

- **Don't feed the animals.** Chipmunks, squirrels, deer, geese, ducks, and other creatures will not benefit from becoming accustomed to handouts from humans.

Scenic Hudson also prohibits motorized vehicles and watercraft, camping, campfires, swimming, hunting (except with a permit in season), horseback riding, smoking, consuming alcohol, use of metal detectors, and use of any sound-transmitting device such as a radio.

YOUR SAFETY: THE TEN ESSENTIALS

Any time you step out on a trail, you may encounter situations that require an abrupt change of plans. Maybe you miss a turn and find yourself lost in the wilderness. Perhaps a storm front moves in without warning, or someone in your party sustains an injury. Any of these circumstances can extend your time outdoors, turning a day hike into an overnight stay or forcing you to seek cover off-trail.

You're not the first to feel compromised in the backcountry—in fact, it happens often enough that there's a checklist of things you should have with you every time you hike. The list is known as the Ten Essentials, items that can help you take control of your situation and make it back home in one piece. It was first developed by the Mountaineers, a club for hikers and climbers, back in the 1930s; they've since updated it in their book *Mountaineering: The Freedom of the Hills*, in which they group some individual items to provide a more thorough list.

If you carry all these things with you on every hike, you'll be ready no matter what nature throws at you.

1. Navigation tools: a good map and compass

2. Sun protection: sunscreen and sunglasses

3. Insulation: extra clothing and a poncho

4. Illumination: Flashlight and/or headlamp

5. First-aid kit

6. Fire starter: lighter and/or waterproof matches

7. Repair kit and tools

8. Nutrition: more food than you think you will need

9. Hydration: more water than you think you will need

10. Emergency shelter: emergency space blanket or ultralight tarp

Keep in mind that while your smartphone may provide maps and a bright light, it will run out of power in the great outdoors and you'll have nowhere to charge it. Equally important, there's no cellular service on most of these hikes, especially those in state parks. If you're going to bring a GPS device with you, choose one that relies on satellites, not on cellular—and bring extra batteries.

NEW YORK CITY AND THE PALISADES

The influence of human industry led to the creation of these hiking experiences in New York, Westchester, and Rockland Counties, as well as in Bergen County, New Jersey. Each of these hikes represents a challenge faced by the expanding metropolis and its drive to provide for its citizens while establishing its place as the country's most important commercial shipping hub.

Fort Lee stands atop the Palisades cliffs, 300-foot-high stands of basalt formed some 200 million years ago during the end-Triassic extinction. These towering walls of rock managed to remain even after railroad companies conducted aggressive quarrying with dynamite in the late 1800s, though formations including Washington Head and Indian Head fell to the blasting. Were it not for the efforts of some local environmentalists to save the iconic walls, the cliffs might have fallen altogether to become railroad ballast.

Railroads thrived nonetheless, and the New York City line carried goods from the docks along the Hudson River to people and companies upstate, and to other lines that moved raw materials and products from overseas into the heart of the Midwest and beyond. When the line's usefulness ended and the elevated railway along Manhattan's 10th Avenue stood permanently idled, enlightened individuals stepped up to create the High Line, a repurposing masterwork.

The Croton Aqueduct brought clean water from reservoirs upstate into every neighborhood of Manhattan from 1842 until 1955. The grassy right-of-way that tops the original structure is now a walking and bicycling trail from Cortlandt to Yonkers, including the dam and waterfall at Croton Gorge.

As you explore this area close to and within the city, you'll see marvels of engineering like the underside of the George Washington Bridge and the exciting neighborhoods springing up around the High Line, and you'll cross through towns filled with history, like Tarrytown, Sleepy Hollow, Dobbs Ferry, and Croton-on-Hudson. If you need a good dose of wilderness after all these man-made marvels, Teatown Lake Reservation provides remarkably quiet surroundings, with a dam-created lake as its picturesque centerpiece.

The Empire State Building is in full view from High Line Park.

1. HIGH LINE PARK

WHY GO?
Relax and enjoy this brilliant repurposing of a railroad line amid a series of reborn city neighborhoods.

THE RUNDOWN

Start: Through the CSX Transportation Gate on West 34th Street near 10th Avenue in midtown Manhattan
Elevation gain: 30 feet (mostly stairs)
Distance: 1.5-mile shuttle (3.0 miles out and back)
Difficulty: Easy
Hiking time: About 1 hour for shuttle (2 hours out and back)
Seasons: Year-round
Schedule: Dec 1–Mar 31: 7 a.m.–7 p.m.; Apr 1–May 31: 7 a.m.–10 p.m.; June 1–Sept 30: 7 a.m.–11 p.m.; Oct 1–Nov 30: 7 a.m.–10 p.m.
Fees and permits: No fees or permits required

Trail contact: Friends of the High Line, 820 Washington St., New York, NY 10014; (212) 500-6035; thehighline.org
Dog-friendly: Service dogs only
Trail surface: Man-made materials
Land status: Friends of the High Line nonprofit conservancy
Nearest town: The trail roughly follows 10th Avenue in the borough of Manhattan, New York City.
Other trail users: Joggers
Maps: USGS: Central Park, NY; trail map available online at thehighline.org/fall-2014-map-1.pdf
Special considerations: The entire trail is accessible to people with disabilities.

FINDING THE TRAILHEAD
The trail is entirely in Manhattan. The northern trailhead (ramp) is on West 34th Street and 10th Avenue. The southern trailhead is at the corner of Gansevoort and Washington Streets in the Meatpacking District (stairs and elevator).
Trailhead GPS: N40 45.382' / W74 00.216'

WHAT TO SEE
A hike in the middle of Manhattan? Thanks to a set of persevering visionaries who saw the potential in a historic freight rail line, the High Line has become a significant highlight of living adjacent to 10th Avenue. Not only is the High Line a well-designed and intelligently crafted elevated walkway, it also has become a magnet for residential and commercial development along its length. This trail serves as a prime example of the power of an outdoor destination to revitalize a neighborhood.

Gardens of native and exotic plants line the High Line walkway.

Built on the obsolete West Side Line of the New York Central Railroad, the High Line project began in 1999 when the nonprofit Friends of the High Line formed with a plan to create an urban green space like the Promenade Plantée in Paris. With advocates including fashion designer Diane von Furstenberg and her husband, media mogul Barry Diller, the Friends gained wide public support for the project and convinced the New York City government, led at the time by Mayor Michael Bloomberg, to commit $50 million to it in 2006. This supplied a major boost to fund-raising efforts, which garnered more than $167 million toward the construction and maintenance of the proposed High Line.

This uncommonly pleasant 1.5-mile trail takes walkers from a point near the Jacob K. Javits Convention Center on 34th Street—where a ramp provides easy access—all the way to Gansevoort Street (3 blocks below 14th Street) in the Meatpacking District. Along the way you'll find a wealth of gardens built into the pathway, favoring native plants that grew alongside the rail tracks or that thrive naturally throughout downstate New York. Exhibits of art commissioned for specific placement on the walkway also grace the route, changing on a more-or-less annual basis. Between the gardens, the art, and the mix of residents and tourists walking with you at any time of day, there's always something fascinating to look at on this trail.

WHAT'S THAT REALLY TALL BUILDING?
Chances are you can pick out One World Trade Center (also known as Free-dom Tower) in downtown Manhattan's financial district—the 1,776-foot build-ing that stands in for the Twin Towers that were destroyed on September 11, 2001. What you may not recognize, however, is the second-tallest building in the city. The skyscraper that stands at 1,396 feet high—the one that seems out of proportion with the rest of its neighborhood—is at 432 Park Avenue, between East 56th and 57th Streets. This building houses 104 condominium apartments, making it the tallest residential building in the world—and, by the way, taller than the original Twin Towers, which topped out at 1,368 feet. Two more condo skyscrapers are expected to open in 2018 at 111 and 217 West 57th Street, so the slender Park Avenue tower will not look so lonely for long.

A glance beyond the railings that line the path, of course, reveals the skyline of Man-hattan and the neighborhoods that have found new life since the High Line arrived. The Gallery District, the Meatpacking District, and Chelsea have seen considerable new construction of both residential and commercial spaces, as well as major galleries like

The High Line repurposes an elevated railway to create a park setting.

the Whitney Museum of American Art, which opened next to the walkway's terminus at Gansevoort Street in 2015. Hudson Yards, a massive redevelopment program that will include as many as sixteen skyscrapers for office, commercial, and residential space, is under construction adjacent to the High Line at the 34th Street end of the route.

If you'd like to know more about the High Line or extend your experience of this trail, visit www.thehighline.org to join a free tour or workshop, or to see if there's a festival or event taking place on the day you plan to visit. You can learn about the horticulture that went into the creation of so many gardens along the trail, find out more about the artists featured there, or perhaps learn how such a project went from a dilapidated railway line to this amazing feat of design and construction.

It's easy to access the High Line by stairs or elevator.

MILES AND DIRECTIONS

0.0 Start at the northern end of the trail. Take the ramp up and walk south.

0.3 Reach a seating area with an art installation.

0.9 Reach 23rd Street Lawn (many plantings).

1.1 Arrive at Chelsea Market Passage (High Line Shop, local vendors, some refreshments).

1.5 Trail ends with overlook onto Gansevoort Street. High Line Shop, restrooms, High Line headquarters in the Diller–von Furstenberg building. (**Option:** Retrace your route for a 3.0-mile round-trip.)

2. FORT LEE HISTORIC PARK: SHORE TRAIL-LONG PATH LOOP

WHY GO?
Follow sweeping views of the Hudson shoreline, including a 320-foot stair climb up the Palisades cliffs.

THE RUNDOWN

Start: Parking area in Fort Lee Historic Park
Elevation gain: 343 feet
Distance: 2.8-mile loop
Difficulty: Strenuous
Hiking time: About 2 hours
Seasons: Spring through fall
Schedule: Open daily dawn to dusk
Fees and permits: Fee for parking at Fort Lee Historic Park
Trail contact: Palisades Interstate Park Commission, 1 Alpine Approach Rd., Alpine, NJ 07620; (201) 768-1360; njpalisades.org/fortlee.html
Dog-friendly: Dogs permitted on the trail; not permitted in Fort Lee Historic Park

Trail surface: Macadam, concrete, dirt/crushed stone, solid-stone steps
Land status: Palisades Interstate Park Commission in New York and New Jersey
Nearest town: Fort Lee, New Jersey
Other trail users: Automobile traffic on road portions
Maps: NatGeo TOPO! Map (USGS): Yonkers, NY; trail map available from the New York–New Jersey Trail Conference: nynjtc.org
Special considerations: This trail includes a 320-foot ascent on roughly 300 uneven stone stairs.

FINDING THE TRAILHEAD

From New York City, take US 9 south to exit 73 for Hudson Terrace in Fort Lee. Continue on Hudson Terrace to Fort Lee Historic Park, and turn left into the park.

From the north, take the Palisades Interstate Parkway south to New Jersey. Continue to the I-95/George Washington Bridge exit, and keep right onto Hudson Terrace in Fort Lee. Continue to Fort Lee Historic Park.

Trailhead GPS: N40 51.094' / W73 57.771'

WHAT TO SEE

At the far southern end of Palisades Interstate Park in northern New Jersey, there's a relatively easy trail that takes you down to the shoreline of the Hudson River. Looking straight across the water, you have a view of the Manhattan skyline in a place where you can linger, sit on a granite bench, and savor the details of this iconic sight. Then, after a

Follow the Hudson
River shoreline on this
New Jersey path.

stroll under the George Washington Bridge, all you have to do is climb some 300 steps to get back to the top of the Palisades cliffs.

Are you up for a challenge? The Carpenter's Trail Loop, as it is known in the park, features a segment of the turquoise-blazed Long Path, a footpath that begins in Altamont, outside Albany, and ends at the George Washington Bridge in Fort Lee, New Jersey—in essence, exactly where you will be on this hike. Developed and maintained by the New

UNDER THE BRIDGE

This trail passes directly under the George Washington Bridge, affording a view usually seen only by area residents who picnic at the foot of the 570-foot steel tower. Here on the New Jersey side, the massive bridge's four main cables are anchored in the Palisades along the river—an operation that required workers to excavate some 200,000 cubic yards of solid rock, according to the Port Authority of New York and New Jersey. This engineering marvel has stood here since 1931, when it first opened to public traffic—more than 5.5 million vehicles drove over the bridge in its first year alone. Today more than 103 million cars, trucks, motorcycles, and other vehicles cross the bridge annually, a number so staggering that *American Infrastructure* magazine named it the world's busiest bridge.

Originally, engineer Othmar Ammann intended to encase the towers in granite and concrete, but the strictures of the Great Depression made this too costly to complete. In the end, the public response to the striking construction of the towers was so positive that Ammann and his team decided to leave the steel exposed. Consider this as you examine the towers up close—especially if you happen to take this hike in the evening, when 380 metal halide lights illuminate the steel.

You won't find a better view of the George Washington Bridge.

York–New Jersey Trail Conference, the 347-mile Long Path crosses the Catskill and Shawangunk Mountains, climbing to 4,000 feet in the Catskill forests and descending through hills and salt marshes to its terminus in northern New Jersey. Keep an eye out for the "parakeet aqua" shade that has become the path's trademark—you will see it on many trails in this book as we cross paths with it in the Hudson Highlands.

You'll find the Long Path at the top of the Palisades cliffs, and there's a significant obstacle between you and it. To reach the top, you'll climb what locals call "The Thousand Steps of Fort Lee," a switchback-filled staircase of uneven stone steps, with a change in elevation of 320 feet.

Generations of Fort Lee residents have climbed up and down these stairs and passed through the two medieval-style tunnels that run under Henry Hudson Drive since they were constructed in 1931. Palisades Interstate Park acquired this land from Carpenter Brothers Company, which operated a huge quarry here, in 1901. The park maintained a series of trails from the top of the ridge to the beach for years, including construction of extensive wooden stairways as park attendance grew. The stone steps and tunnels made the walk down from the cliff easier, eliminating the need to cross roads to reach the river, picnic areas, and beach below.

More than a century has passed since then, and time, age, and weather have worn away surfaces and forced cracks in the original masonry. This trail continues to require substantial maintenance and repair. Palisades Interstate Park museum technician Eric Nelsen tells me that the latest big round of work on it was in 2012. In some places chunks of rock have broken off the stairs, making them uneven and not especially flat. The steps also do not match building codes for height and size, so you may have to lift your feet a good 12 inches or more to make it to the next tread. That being said, Nic and I made it up these stairs on a hot day in early June, and I know some people reading this are thinking, "That sounds awesome!" If you like a good challenge and a sense of walking in the footsteps of history—literally, in this case—you will love this hike.

If climbing all these stairs sounds like too big a challenge even before you start, you can always take the trail in the opposite direction and go down the stairs instead of up. You'll still climb some stairs on the other end of the beach as you return to street level, but these are not nearly as intimidating as the angles, twists, and turns of the "Thousand Stairs."

MILES AND DIRECTIONS

0.0 Start on the north side of the bus parking area in Fort Lee Historic Park. Follow the macadam path; watch for the turquoise (Long Path) and white (Shore Trail) blazes.

0.2 Follow the sidewalk. At the bottom of the stairs, follow the blazes right to Hudson Terrace. At the park entrance, turn left. Follow the white blazes on utility poles along the macadam path.

0.6 At Henry Hudson Drive, look left past the parkway exit for the sign for the Shore Trail. Turn left and take the dirt path next to the road.

Stone tunnels lead under Henry Hudson Drive.

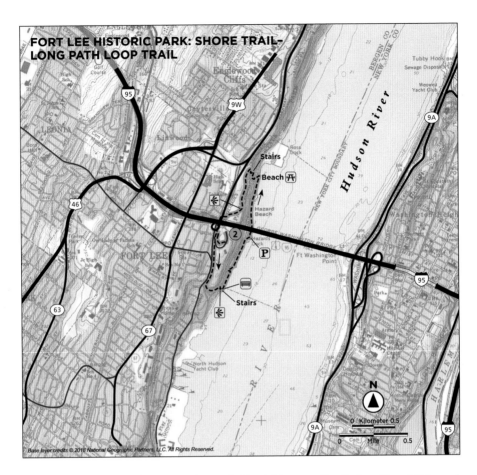

0.7 Enjoy a view of upper Manhattan to the right, across the Hudson River. Start down the rock stairs.

0.8 At the landing, turn left. Continue down the stairs. At the bottom of the stairs, you're on the Shore Trail. There are granite benches here. The George Washington Bridge is to the north.

1.2 Reach the parking area at the base of the George Washington Bridge.

1.4 Come to the end of parking area. Continue straight on the road.

1.7 Carpenters Trail (blue blaze) appears on left. Take the stairs up. The ascent here is 320 feet on stairs. The stairs go up to two tunnels and then continue after the tunnels.

2.0 At the top of the stairs, turn left for Fort Lee, following the blue blazes south.

2.2 Come to an overlook to the left. You're now following the Long Path (turquoise blazes). Continue straight.

2.4 Take a footbridge over a ramp to the George Washington Bridge, then stairs down to the road. At the bottom of the stairs, turn left and walk up Hudson Terrace, following the Long Path blazes on utility poles. Continue to the Fort Lee entrance.

2.6 Climb up the concrete stairs (these are regulation size), and continue to the parking area.

2.8 Arrive back at the trailhead.

3. CROTON GORGE PARK

WHY GO?
Natural wonder and man-made marvels meet on this easy stroll at the top of the Old Croton Aqueduct.

THE RUNDOWN

Start: Parking area at the base of Croton Dam
Elevation gain: 118 feet
Distance: 1.6-mile loop
Difficulty: Easy
Hiking time: About 1 hour
Seasons: Year-round
Schedule: Open 8 a.m. to dusk
Fees and permits: Parking fee (reduced fee with park pass) May–Sept, Fri–Sun; free parking on weekdays and Oct–Apr
Trail contact: Westchester County Parks; (914) 827-9568; parks .westchestergov.com

Dog-friendly: Dogs permitted on leash
Trail surface: Dirt, some paved sections
Land status: Westchester County park
Nearest town: Cortlandt, New York
Other trail users: Cross-country skiers in season
Maps: NatGeo TOPO! Map (USGS): Ossining, NY; Croton Gorge Unique Area map available online at dec.ny .gov/lands/96697.html

FINDING THE TRAILHEAD
From Cortlandt, take NY 129 south and east to 35 Yorktown Rd. The park is on your left (east).
From the south, take US 9 north to Croton-on-Hudson; then take NY 129 east and north to the park at 35 Yorktown Rd. (on your right).
Trailhead GPS: N41 13.575' / W73 51.453'

WHAT TO SEE
The first large masonry dam in the United States stood near here in Croton Gorge, at the northernmost point in New York City's original water transport system. Here the Old Croton Aqueduct began, completed in 1842 and used to bring clean, fresh water into the city until late in the nineteenth century. The 40.5-mile aqueduct and the original dam became prototypes for many other cities and regions to follow, including the present-day Catskill and Delaware water system, which supplies 90 percent of New York City's water today.

The dam and aqueduct solved a significant sanitation problem for the thriving metropolis, which had attempted to make do with cisterns, springs, and wells for hundreds of years. The lack of availability of fresh water had turned some neighborhoods in

The New Croton Dam was constructed in 1906.

Walk to the top of the dam for magnificent views.

Manhattan into hotbeds of disease—particularly Five Points in Lower Manhattan, the most notorious slum in the world by the 1830s. When a cholera epidemic ran rampant through the city and killed more than 3,500 people in a single year, city leaders created the Board of Water Commissioners to solve the problem. In 1837 construction began on the aqueduct and the dam in Croton Gorge.

What you see here is actually the second dam, completed in 1906 and dubbed the New Croton Dam, a name that sticks more than a century later. Its official name is the Cornell Dam, however, named for A. B. Cornell, who relinquished his land for the construction of this edifice. To create a much larger reservoir than the original 50-foot-high dam could contain, workers on the project dug a 1,000-foot-long canal to reroute the river, lining this canal with masonry and using a series of interim dams to move the river's flow. It took eight years to complete this task, and another six to stage extensive repairs to keep the river in check, according to the Historic American Engineering Record in the Library of Congress.

Rising nearly 300 feet and presenting an imposing 266-foot width, the dam's base begins 130 feet below the Croton River's bed. The result is a spillway that creates a powerful waterfall, while the dam holds back up to 19 billion gallons of water in a man-made lake that covers what was once Cornell's property, as well as hundreds of other farms in the area. This is still just a fraction of New York City's modern-day requirements, but

From the top of the dam, watch the Croton River flow on its way to the Bronx.

at the time the city depended on this reservoir and the aqueduct to provide most of its water supply—and the dam and aqueduct delivered, sending 200 to 300 million gallons of water each day to the Jerome Park Reservoir in the northern Bronx.

WHO BUILT THE DAM?

As with most major construction projects in the nineteenth and twentieth centuries, immigrants made up the workforce for the New Croton Dam. Superintendent of Excavation John B. Goldsborough first called on the men who had built the original dam fifty years before, but the able-bodied young masons he had known were now men in their 70s, and the hard labor involved in erecting the dam soon overwhelmed them.

Goldsborough needed skilled masons, so he reached overseas to southern Italy, recruiting professionals who believed they were coming to America to seek their fortunes—leaving their families behind but planning to send for them later. However, when the Italian recruits arrived at Staten Island, they boarded a train for the new dam site, where they found that they would be living in shacks built on stilts—and working for wages too small to live on comfortably, much less send money home to their families.

This workforce excavated the riverbed, built a canal in the hillside to divert the river water, and began construction of the new dam; but the long hours of backbreaking work, starvation wages, and miserable living conditions eventually took their toll. On April 1, 1900, the quarrymen put down their tools and went on strike; all the other artisans and laborers on the job joined them. The National Guard arrived to continue the work, but New York City Mayor Seth Low heeded the men's complaints about working conditions. He pushed through legislation to create the mandatory 8-hour workday in New York.

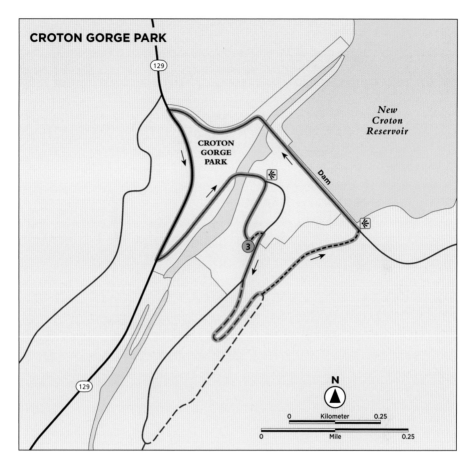

CROTON GORGE PARK

129

New
Croton
Reservoir

CROTON
GORGE
PARK

Dam

3

129

N

0   Kilometer   0.25

0   Mile   0.25

Your hiking experience here is fairly easy, with one long, gradual incline to the top of the dam, where a recently reconstructed bridge provides a particularly striking viewpoint for the spillway waterfall, the reservoir, and the rerouted Croton River. To form a loop, we took a short walk along NY 129, leaving the park for about 0.2 mile. You may choose to forfeit this brief period along the highway and simply go back the way you came, enjoying a more leisurely and less nerve-wracking route through the park and to your vehicle.

MILES AND DIRECTIONS

0.0   Start from the parking area and enjoy the "wow!" view of Croton Dam and its waterfall. When you're ready, cross the bridge over the Croton River in front of the dam.

0.2   Take the trail that begins at the west end of the parking area.

0.3   The trail splits. On the left is the Old Croton Aqueduct Trail and the trail to the dam. Go left.

0.5   The Old Croton Aqueduct Trail goes back and to the right. Go straight to continue to the dam.

0.7   Reach the top of the dam. There's a great view of the reservoir to the east and the Croton River to the west.

1.2   At the north end of the dam, you can see the length of the spillway and how the water rejoins the Croton River. Cross the bridge here and continue on the road (NY 129). The shoulder is narrow; walk on the left, facing traffic. (**Option:** To avoid the on-road section, retrace your steps for a 2.4-mile out-and-back hike.)

1.4   Turn left to reenter the park.

1.6   Arrive back at the parking area.

4. OLD CROTON AQUEDUCT TRAIL: SCARBOROUGH TO SLEEPY HOLLOW

WHY GO?

Follow the course of New York City's original water source on a shady trail through lush woodland with occasional dashes of history.

THE RUNDOWN

Start: Parking area to the left of the road, across from Clear View School in Scarborough

Elevation gain: 259 feet

Distance: 3.6-mile shuttle (7.2 miles out and back)

Difficulty: Easy

Hiking time: About 1.5 hours (3 hours round-trip)

Seasons: Year-round

Schedule: Open daily dawn to dusk

Fees and permits: No fees or permits required

Trail contact: Old Croton Aqueduct State Historic Park, 15 Walnut St., Dobbs Ferry, NY 10522; (914) 693-5259 or (914) 631-1470; nysparks .state.ny.us/parks/96/details.aspx

Dog-friendly: Dogs permitted on leash

Trail surface: Dirt and mowed-grass path

Land status: New York state historic park

Nearest town: Scarborough and Sleepy Hollow, New York

Other trail users: Trail runners, cyclists, equestrians; cross-country skiers in season

Maps: NatGeo TOPO! Map (USGS): Ossining, NY; trail map available to order (fee) at aqueduct.org

FINDING THE TRAILHEAD

From the north or south, take the Thruway (I-87 North) to exit 9 (Tarrytown/ Sleepy Hollow/US 9 North). Travel north on US 9 for 4.6 miles to River Road in Briarcliff Manor. Turn left on River Road and immediately park in the parking area to the left of the road, across from Clear View School. GPS: N41 07.832' / W73 51.671'

To reach the second parking area at the end of the hike, from exit 9 on I-87, travel north on US 9 to Bedford Road in Sleepy Hollow. Turn right on Bedford Road and continue to the Sleepy Hollow High School parking area. GPS: N41 05.212' / W73 51.35'

Trailhead GPS: N41 07.832' / W73 51.671'

WHAT TO SEE

One of the area's oldest and most established walking trails, the Old Croton Aqueduct Trail connects the Lower Hudson Valley with Yonkers and the Bronx by following the

You will see three ventilators like this one on this section of the Croton Aqueduct Trail.

route of New York City's first transported water supply. Pedestrians, cyclists, and horseback riders now travel along the top of the aqueduct, an underground brick tunnel 8½ feet high and 7½ feet wide. Your hike takes you atop the protective covering of earth that shields the aqueduct from the elements, allowing this remarkable feat of engineering to carry clean water from Croton Dam all the way to the center of New York, where it filled reservoirs on the sites of today's Great Lawn in Central Park and the New York Public Library.

Construction of the aqueduct began in 1837, and it began transporting water on June 22, 1842, through its underground corridor of stone, brick, and hydraulic cement. Shaped like a horseshoe, the conduit transported about 72 million gallons of water into the city daily, following the route workers had created by cutting through hills, filling in valleys, and keeping the entire aqueduct on a trajectory that dropped by just 13.25 inches per mile. It flowed through 16 tunnels, followed 114 culverts, and continued its pace over a large arch bridge constructed over the Sing Sing Kill in Ossining. The aqueduct even crossed the Harlem River, where a bridge resembling the aqueducts designed by the Romans supported the masonry conduit.

The aqueduct remained reliable for decades, with engineers making modifications to increase its capacity to 90 million gallons per day, but it could not keep pace with New York City's exponential growth rate. The city's population tripled between 1840 and 1870 as immigrants from Europe poured into Castle Garden, took jobs in the city, and did their best to make new homes for themselves and their families in downtown Manhattan and Brooklyn. New York needed a much larger aqueduct to provide water to all these people, so construction got under way in 1885 to create the New Croton Aqueduct—a system with a 340-million-gallon daily capacity.

Old Croton Aqueduct continued to function and was finally retired in 1965 (although parts of it still bring water to Ossining), but its subterranean passageways still stand, descending slightly more than 13 inches per mile along the aqueduct's 41-mile length. The surface level served as an informal walkway for local and long-distance pedestrians throughout the aqueduct's history. Today, Old Croton Aqueduct State Historic Park provides excellent strolling, cycling, and hiking opportunities to tens of thousands of area residents each year. The American Society of Civil Engineers has dubbed Old Croton Aqueduct a National Historic Civil Engineering Landmark. The original aqueduct is on the National Register of Historic Places, and it also stands as a National Historic Landmark.

This hike provides a sampling of the trail's numerous scenic and historical attributes. You'll pass three ventilators, cylindrical stone towers that allow fresh air to circulate over

Part of the trail passes through Rockefeller State Park Preserve.

The weir stands where the aqueduct crosses the Pocantico River.

the water below. This trail segment crosses the Archville Bridge, which reconnected segments of the trail after a seventy-four-year severance. Perhaps best of all, you will pass through Sleepy Hollow—a real place after all—where author Washington Irving penned his classic tale of Ichabod Crane and the Headless Horseman. Irving's remains are interred in the Sleepy Hollow Cemetery (as are those of legendary industrialist and philanthropist Andrew Carnegie), a stop worthy of a detour from the main trail.

MILES AND DIRECTIONS

0.0 Start from the parking area on River Road in Scarborough, and begin walking south on the aqueduct trail. The path is mowed here, with a narrow, bare dirt trail running down the middle. There's a neighborhood just beyond the wooded area to your right.

0.2 Reach #10 ventilator.

0.4 Note the trail markers (the first you've seen) here. These State of New York Taconic Region markers are white plastic disks with black ink. The trail turns right here; you'll walk a short paved portion past a private home. Soon the trail bears left, bisecting this private property. Continue on the trail to Country Club Road. Cross the road and continue straight on the trail.

0.8 A connecting trail goes right here. Bear left. The trail becomes a wide, crushed-stone path through a lovely wooded area. You'll see many Asian wineberry bushes along the trail; these bear fruit in July, and you're welcome to sample.

0.9 Reach the Archville Bridge. A stone marker here notes that the aqueduct's first arch over a road—Broadway in this case—was completed here in 1839. In a moment you'll come to #11 ventilator.

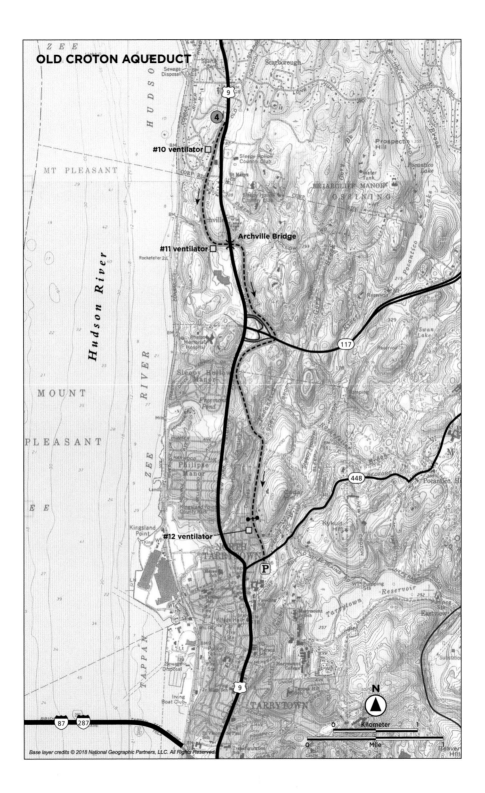

OLD CROTON AQUEDUCT

#10 ventilator

Archville Bridge

#11 ventilator

#12 ventilator

HUDSON RIVER

Hudson River

ZEE RIVER

TAPPAN

MOUNT

PLEASANT

MT PLEASANT

N

1.8 A loop trail goes to the left here. Follow the green signposts for the "OCA" and turn right. Cross the bridge over NY 117. After the bridge, take the first trail to your right. You're now passing through Rockefeller State Park Preserve. Access to the preserve is free from here. You'll see short blue posts that indicate intersections between the preserve's 55 miles of carriage roads and the Old Croton Aqueduct Trail.

2.7 Another trail crosses the aqueduct trail. Continue straight. Sleepy Hollow Cemetery is on your right. In about 50 steps you'll come to a weir, a large masonry edifice that contains a metal gate. When the aqueduct required maintenance, operators could lower the gate to divert the flow of water through the tunnel. Weirs were used at river crossings—the aqueduct crosses the Pocantico River here.

3.3 As you approach the wrought-iron gate ahead, the Hudson River and the Tappan Zee Bridge come into view on your right. Pass around the right side of the gate and cross Brook Road. The trail continues across the street.

3.4 Reach #12 ventilator.

3.6 Cross Bedford Road to the Sleepy Hollow High School parking area. If you are walking back to the beginning of the hike, this is your turnaround point. If you parked a car here, your hike has come to an end. You'll find many good places for lunch in Sleepy Hollow or just south in Tarrytown.

5. TEATOWN LAKE RESERVATION

WHY GO?

Quiet in the midst of suburban hubbub, this walk through a natural area will soothe your city-weary senses.

THE RUNDOWN

Start: In the northwest corner of the alternate parking area on Spring Valley Road

Elevation gain: 108 feet

Distance: 1.7-mile loop

Difficulty: Easy

Hiking time: About 1.25 hours

Seasons: Year-round

Schedule: Trails open daily, dawn to dusk

Fees and permits: No fees or permits required

Trail contact: Teatown Lake Reservation, 1600 Spring Valley Rd., Ossining, NY 10562; (914) 762-2912; teatown.org

Dog-friendly: Dogs permitted on leash (Please clean up after your pet.) Professional dog walkers with more than two dogs are not allowed.

Trail surface: Crushed stone, dirt, boardwalks

Land status: Permanently protected through a private land conservancy

Nearest town: Ossining, New York

Other trail users: Joggers; cross-country skiers, snowshoers in season

Maps: NatGeo TOPO! Map (USGS): Ossining, NY; trail map available at the nature center and online at teatown.org/wp-content/uploads/2016/11/Teatown-Lake-Reservation-Trail-Map.pdf

FINDING THE TRAILHEAD

From Ossining, head north on US 9 to Cedar Lane. Bear right on Cedar Lane and continue for 1.7 miles until Cedar becomes Spring Valley Road. Continue 2.1 miles on Spring Valley Road to 1600 Spring Valley Rd. in Teatown.

From the north, take US 9 to Crotonville (Yorktown). In Crotonville, turn left onto Ogden Road and continue as it becomes Spring Valley Road. Continue 3.4 miles on Spring Valley Road to 1600 Spring Valley Rd. in Teatown.

Trailhead GPS: N41 12.653' / W73 49.597'

WHAT TO SEE

Back in 1776, on the eve of the Revolutionary War, a man named John Arthur saw an opportunity to capitalize on the scarcity of tea in the area north of New York City. Since the Boston Tea Party in 1775, when patriots dumped an entire shipment of tea into Boston Harbor to protest high taxation, England had held back its tea exports, leaving Americans to scramble to find some or go without. Arthur had somehow come by a chest of tea, perhaps horded since the tea crisis began. He intended to sell it to the people

Mayapple is one of the spring blooms at Teatown Lake Reservation.

of New York at exorbitant fees, lining his own pockets with the spoils.

Arthur did not expect the Daughters of Eve, however, and when this group of activist women came knocking on his door one day, he balked at their demand that he lower the price of his tea. When he refused to negotiate, the Daughters surrounded his house and placed him under siege so that he could neither leave to sell his tea or allow customers to approach his home. Finally, exhausted and undone by the whole ordeal, Arthur relented. He sold the rest of his tea at a reasonable price, and the locals dubbed his land "Teatown"—a name that has lasted through the centuries.

After John Arthur's ownership ended, a sequence of owners purchased and protected the land, building the stables and carriage house and riding their horses over the countryside. The last of these was Gerald Swope, whose fortune came through his chairmanship of General Electric. He built horse trails, stabling his family's horses in the English Tudor buildings that now house the Teatown Nature Center and offices. Swope dammed Bailey Brook to create Teatown Lake, a 42-acre pond that covers a former meadow.

Swope and his family lived here for more than thirty years, and his children inherited the land when he died in 1957. They, in turn, gifted the land to the Brooklyn

The boardwalk offers expansive views of the lake.

The easy, level trail at Teatown leads through shady woods.

Botanic Garden, with the stipulation that it be preserved as open space with educational tools that would teach the public about the importance of conserving areas such as this one. Today this lovely property functions independently of the Brooklyn Botanic Garden, with expanded holdings of more than 1,000 acres and delightful opportunities for observing wildlife, learning about native plants, and getting some much-needed solitude and exercise just minutes from the nation's most-populous metropolis.

I chose the Lakeside Loop trail to follow through the reservation to provide an introductory overview of the property, but you will find many other options as you wander. The Twin Lakes Loop, for example, leads to lakes that are farther into the wilderness

WILDFLOWER ISLAND: AN OASIS OF NATIVE PLANTS

When Gerald Swope decided to dam Bailey Brook to make Teatown Lake, he accidentally surrounded one area of high farmland with brook water. This former hilltop became an island—and because it sat alone in the lake, the invasive plants that would one day infiltrate much of Teatown Lake Reservation could not reach across the water to this isolated spot.

The land stewards who managed this land beginning in 1962 recognized the opportunity this little island provided to raise native plants that struggled to survive on the mainland amid invasive species like multiflora rose, garlic mustard, and Tatarian honeysuckle. In 1982 Teatown education director Warren Balgooyen worked with Marjorie Swope to create Wildflower Island, a laboratory for the study of native plants and a place for visitors to learn about the wildflowers, trees, and shrubs that should be growing in downstate New York. You can take a guided tour of this remarkable island; check teatown.org/visitors/wildflower-island/ to see when tours are scheduled.

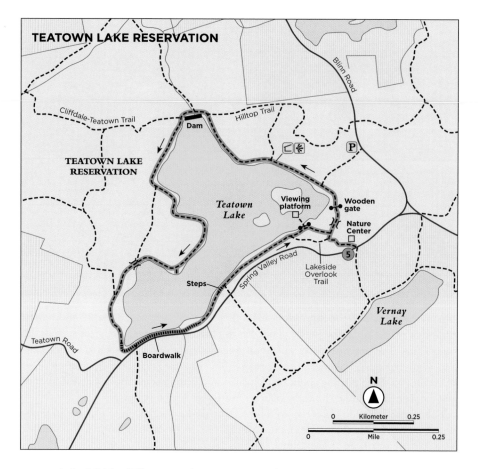

area; and the Hidden Valley Loop brings you to other areas of meadow and shrubland. You may find the Cliffdale-Teatown Trail more challenging if you're looking to get your heart pumping. Pick up a map at the nature center before your hike to see if you'd like to explore the more remote areas of the preserve.

MILES AND DIRECTIONS

0.0 Start in the northwest corner of the paved parking area, and go through a wooden gate. Follow the signs for the Lakeside Trail (blue markers). At the Y junction, bear right and take the stone steps down. Turn right at the bottom and cross the bridge. The Wildflower Woods trail goes left; continue straight.

0.1 Here's another wooden gate; go through. Pass junctions for connectors to the Hilltop and Hidden Valley Trails.

0.3 A shelter provides a nice view of the lake. The trail splits in a moment; bear left. Watch for evidence of beaver activity in this area.

0.5 The Hilltop Loop goes right. Continue left on the Lakeside Trail to the dam. Pass junctions for the Teatown, Kitchawan, and Hilltop Trails; continue along the dam and around it to the left.

0.6 An access trail to the power lines goes right here. Continue left.

1.0 Cross a bridge.

1.1 The Hilltop Trail goes right; the Lakeside and Briarcliff-Peekskill Trails go left. Continue left.

1.2 Turn left as the 0.1-mile boardwalk begins.

1.4 Reach a short section of stone steps.

1.5 A wooden gate leads to a viewing platform. This is the bridge to Wildflower Island (access by appointment only). Take the path across from the island's interpretive sign to return to the parking area.

1.7 Arrive back at the parking area.

6. PIERMONT MARSH AND PIER

WHY GO?

Two for the price of one: This hike combines a leisurely stroll straight out into the Hudson River with a close examination of a challenged marsh.

THE RUNDOWN

Start: Parking area on Ferry Road east of Paradise Avenue in the town of Piermont

Elevation gain: 62 feet

Distance: 3.6 miles round-trip, including two out-and-back trails and a short connecting walk between them

Difficulty: Easy

Hiking time: 1.5 to 1.75 hours

Seasons: Spring through fall

Schedule: Open daily, dawn to dusk

Fees and permits: No fees or permits required

Trail contact: NYS Department of Environmental Conservation, Hudson River Research Reserve, 256 Norrie Point Way, PO Box 315, Staatsburg, NY 12580; (845) 889-4745; e-mail: hrnerr@dec.ny.gov

Dog-friendly: Dogs permitted on leash

Trail surface: Paved (Piermont Pier); sidewalk and crushed gravel (Piermont Marsh path)

Land status: New York State Department of Environmental Conservation

Nearest town: Piermont, New York

Other trail users: Bicyclists, strollers, joggers

Maps: NatGeo TOPO! Map (USGS): Nyack, NY; Piermont Marsh map available online at dec.ny.gov/docs/remediation_hudson_pdf/piermont.pdf

Special considerations: Park once at the lot for Piermont Pier (see above) and walk along town sidewalks between these trailheads. Do not drive down the pier; a permit is required, and fines for driving on the pier without a permit are steep.

FINDING THE TRAILHEAD

From the Palisades Interstate Parkway, take exit 5S and merge onto NY 303 South toward Tappan. Turn left onto Kings Highway. In 0.9 mile, turn right onto Orangeburg Road, which soon becomes Piermont Avenue and then Valentine Avenue. Turn left onto Ferndon Avenue and continue to Paradise Avenue. Turn right on Paradise and then bear left onto Ferry Avenue. Turn right to stay on Ferry Avenue; park in the parking area on your left.

Trailhead GPS: N41 02.438' / W73 54.683'

WHAT TO SEE

At just over 1,000 acres, Piermont Marsh stretches for 2 miles along the bank of the Hudson River at a point where Atlantic Ocean salt water meets inland freshwater to

Piermont Pier is a popular place at sunset in spring and summer.

See the new Mario Cuomo bridge from Piermont Pier.

create a brackish tidal marsh. Sparkill Creek runs through this wetland, providing the only real access to the interior of this unique wilderness area on the edge of Tallman Mountain State Park; but you can get a close look at the enormity and the edges of Pier-mont Marsh on this pair of trails.

While the Hudson River hosts salt marshes farther downstream, freshwater from the river's northern reaches in the Adirondacks and from natural watersheds along its length eventually meet the salt water pushed upstream by the ocean's tides. This creates a tran-sitional marsh, home to a variety of plants that can only grow in a brackish environment. Unfortunately, such marshes may be dominated by nonnative species like Japanese knot-weed and phragmites—the tall plants with the tassel at the top—which eventually crowd out native species. That's the case in Piermont Marsh, and the Hudson River National Estuarine Research Reserve (HRNERR) is working to learn as much as possible about changes in the marsh over the past several decades and about what can be done to restore the native plants that compete for survival here.

HRNERR is working with the New York State Department of Environmental Con-servation to develop a long-term strategy for the management of Piermont Marsh. Inva-sive species are only the most visible challenge the marsh faces—as sea levels rise, the composition of the entire marsh may change. Piermont Marsh provides protection for the village of Piermont from major storms, but this ability could be lost as climate change and other factors take their toll on the Atlantic shoreline, the river and all its tributaries, and the marshes that line the riverbanks.

This hike provides two enlightening views of this remarkable place: an open view of the entire 2-mile length of the marsh from Piermont Pier and a close-up study along a section of the Tallman Mountain State Park bicycle path. The pier takes you some distance into the Hudson River itself, and, depending on the height of the tide, you may see the remains of wooden docks that once lined the pier. Each season brings a different variety of waterfowl: Canada geese, mute swans, American black ducks, double-crested

THE CASE AGAINST PHRAGMITES

The tall plant stalks that crowd together in this and many other marshes across America have become so familiar to hikers and nature lovers that they seem to belong here. They are part of a genus (plant category) known as *Phragmites*, specifically the species *Phragmites australis*, and they arrived here from Europe hundreds of years ago. They look markedly similar to an American species, *Phragmites americanus*, but the European species is much hardier and prevents the native plant from populating the marshes. *P. australis* has the capacity to grow quickly in large colonies, blocking out sunlight for any species not as tall or hardy. Marshes across the country have become vast monocultures of this aggressive plant, leaving little hope for survival of the other plants that birds, animals, and fish require to live and breed. The challenge for estuarine scien-tists is to find a way to defeat *P. australis* before it obliterates all other plants that belong in this marsh—and, perhaps, restore the marsh to its original condi-tion. This could bring back the birds and animals that once thrived here, like the muskrat and tall wading birds, including herons and egrets.

Canada geese and other waterfowl raise their young in Piermont Marsh.

cormorants, and mallards teaching their young to swim in summer; spring and fall migrations of ring-necked ducks and redheads; and rafts of overwintering ducks including scaup, bufflehead, ruddy duck, and canvasback. Rockland Audubon reports that many rarities find their way to Piermont Marsh as well, so keep an eye out for species like American avocet, red-throated loon, sandwich and royal terns, Franklin's gull, and smaller birds like grasshopper and seaside sparrows.

MILES AND DIRECTIONS

0.0 Start from the parking area on Ferry Road, and head east on the wide paved road.

0.4 Reach the Hudson River. The Tappan Zee Bridge is north of you.

0.9 You've reached the end of the pier. Return the way you came.

1.8 Continue on Ferry Road past the parking area, and turn left as the road does. Walk down Ferry Road on the sidewalk to the large parking area.

1.9 Arrive at a large parking lot. Continue to the Piermont Marsh interpretive area.

2.0 Come to the interpretive display for Piermont Marsh. Make a stop here, and then continue on the sidewalk. At Pvt. Richard Fournier Street, cross to your

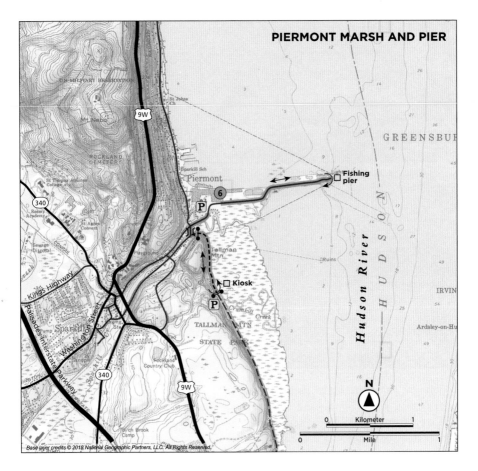

PIERMONT MARSH AND PIER

left and continue on the sidewalk up Richard Fournier Street (past the Kane Park Playground). If you wish, stop at the playground to enjoy the overlook.

2.2 Cross the bridge over Sparkill Creek. After the bridge, there's a gravel path on your left with a yellow gate. Turn left onto this path.

2.4 Reach the end of the bike path in this part of Tallman Mountain State Park. There's a gate here, followed by a public pool. The marsh is to your left. Continue straight across the parking area.

2.6 There's a Piermont Marsh information kiosk across from the pool. This is a nice spot from which to view the expanse of the marsh.

2.7 There's a dirt road here at the south end of the parking area, if you'd like a longer hike. Otherwise, turn around and return the way you came.

3.6 Arrive back at the parking area.

7. ANTHONY'S NOSE

[icon]

WHY GO?

A short, steep climb to one of the finest views in the Hudson Valley.

THE RUNDOWN

Start: Parking area off US 6/202 on the edge of Broccy Creek (*not* at the Bear Mountain Toll House, but the next parking area as you head north up the hill toward the Bear Mountain Bridge)
Elevation gain: 569 feet
Distance: 2.6 miles out and back
Difficulty: Strenuous
Hiking time: About 2.5 hours
Seasons: Spring through fall
Schedule: Open daily, dawn to dusk
Fees and permits: No fees or permits required
Trail contact: Hudson Highlands State Park Preserve, 1498 Route 301, Carmel, NY 10512; (845) 225-7207; parks.ny.gov/parks/9/hunting.aspx
Dog-friendly: Dogs permitted on leash

Trail surface: Dirt and woodland detritus
Land status: New York state park
Nearest town: Peekskill, New York
Other trail users: Hikers only
Maps: NatGeo TOPO! Map (USGS): Peekskill, NY; NatGeo Trails Illustrated Map #756: Harriman, Bear Mountain, Sterling Forest State Parks; #1508: Appalachian Trail, Delaware Water Gap to Schaghticoke Mountain; New York–New Jersey Trail Conference Trail Map #101: East Hudson Trails
Special considerations: You can make this a shuttle hike by parking one car at this trailhead and one at the Appalachian Trail parking area on NY 9D on the north side of the mountain. GPS: N41 32.2571' / W73 97.5949'

FINDING THE TRAILHEAD

From Cold Spring, drive north on US 6/202 along the eastern edge of the Hudson River. After passing the Bear Mountain Toll House, watch on your right for another parking area in about 0.5 mile. Pull into this parking area. The trailhead is at the northwest corner of the lot.
Trailhead GPS: N41 18.732' / W73 57.8970'

WHAT TO SEE

At the northernmost part of Westchester County, facing Bear Mountain across the river like a towering, bright green bookend, Anthony's Nose stands as one of the most imposing landmarks in the Hudson Valley, issuing a silent challenge to every hiker who treads the region's trails. Its easy accessibility from three trailheads along NY 9D makes it one of the area's most popular hikes, with parties of eager scenery seekers making their way up the clearly marked trail in any season.

Those who take the trail along the edge of Camp Smith—the New York National Guard training area—and up the Canada Hill granite slopes to the summit deserve a significant reward, and Anthony's Nose delivers just such gratification thanks to its height and vantage point. The view just past the summit may be the finest in the valley—a 270-degree panorama of the river, the Hudson Highlands, Harriman and Bear Mountain State Parks, and the landscape extending well into Putnam and Orange Counties.

Who is Anthony, and why did someone name this proboscis-like promontory for him? The name dates back to the seventeenth century, making it anyone's guess which of the many stories is the true one. The mountain's first European owner, Pierre Van Cortlandt, claimed that the name referred to Anthony Hogan, a sea captain with an oversize beak, the likes of which apparently made him legendary. While sailing up the river, one of the captain's men joked that the protruding point on the east side of the river resembled his superior officer, and the mountain henceforth bore Hogan's name.

Van Cortlandt's influence did not extend beyond his land, however, and other knowledgeable authorities speculated on the mountain's namesake.

Writer Washington Irving, storyteller extraordinaire who penned *The Legend of Sleepy Hollow* and *Rip Van Winkle*, wrote a satire called *A History of New York* in 1809 in which he

Anthony's Nose rises at the end of Bear Mountain Bridge.

Bear Mountain dominates the landscape from atop Anthony's Nose.

posited that the horn player on explorer Henry Hudson's ship earned enough of a reputation to get an entire mountain named for him. Anthony Van Corlaer drew the attention of Peter Stuyvesant, Dutch governor of what was then New Amsterdam, on a night in 1642 when the leader learned that the English were on their way to usurp the Dutch and claim the colony for themselves. Stuyvesant ordered Van Corlaer to run to the colony and play his trumpet to awaken the colonists so they could prepare to defend themselves and their land. The horn player left immediately, but he had to cross the river to reach the colony, and there was no ferryman on this stormy night. The hapless trumpeter threw himself into the river and attempted to swim across . . . but drowned (though some suggest he was eaten by a bull shark). After his death, the mountain became a symbol of Van Corlaer's large, shiny red nose, a prominent feature as memorable as his bravery.

Or perhaps the mountain is named for one of several saints named Anthony, as a counterpoint to an unusual rock formation on Breakneck Ridge once known as Saint Anthony's Face. As this eponymous outcrop was blown to bits during the quarrying era in the 1800s, it's hard to guess what parallels may have been drawn by early settlers between it and the mountain across the river.

A last story suggests that the nose of one of the first colonists, a Dutch Reformed Church deacon named Anthony De Hooges, may have been the inspiration for the mountain's name. De Hooges served the patroonship of Rensselaerswijck, and his

The rugged trail features streams, large rocks, and challenging inclines.

biographer, Dirk Mouw, notes in *The Memorandum Book of Anthony De Hooges* that "some of the earliest mentions of De Hooges made by researchers state (though without providing documentation) that the 'promontory' or 'mountain' which stands near the east landing of the Bear Mountain Bridge over the Hudson River ... was named for De Hooges—enshrining in cartography a facial feature for which he was evidently remembered by those who had known him personally—as 'Anthony's Nose.'"

Whichever tale you wish to believe, we can take one thing away from this slice of history: Back in the 1600s, a lot of people named Anthony seem to be endowed with really large noses. Consider this as you make your way to the top.

MILES AND DIRECTIONS

0.0 Start at the trailhead on NY 9D—you'll see a Fallen Rock Zone sign across from the parking area. (This is *not* the trailhead at the Bear Mountain Toll House—that one is farther east.) At the trailhead, turn left immediately and follow the blue markers. Cross a stream on flat rocks.

0.3 After climbing for a while, look for blue blazes on rocks and double markers to your left. Turn left; cross another stream.

0.5 At the top of a rise, turn right, following the blue markers. The trail rounds a bend and heads left, leveling off for a while.

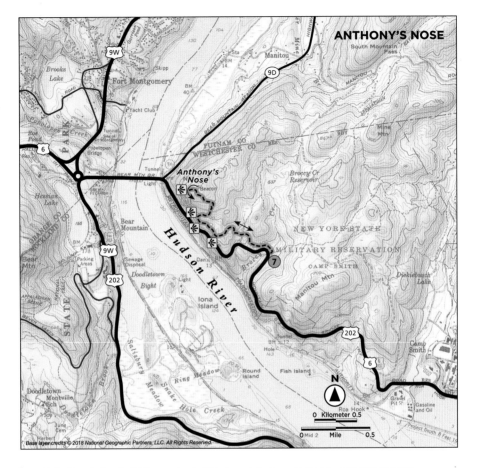

0.6 Reach the first big overlook. This is not Anthony's Nose—you can see the nose to your right. Bear Mountain Bridge is to your left, and a railroad bridge hugs the water to the right. When you're ready, continue straight on the blue trail.

0.8 Reach the second viewpoint. From here the trail climbs. Another viewpoint comes up in a few hundred feet. Bear Mountain is directly across from you here.

1.2 This area of exposed rock is the summit, but there's no view here. Keep going beyond the summit on the blue trail.

1.3 You earned a great view, and here it is—maybe the best in the Hudson Valley. Stop here, unpack your lunch, and enjoy the spectacle. When you're ready, return the way you came.

2.6 Arrive back at the parking area.

PUTNAM AND ORANGE COUNTIES

If you're ready to enjoy the best hiking experiences in New York State, visit the trails in the state parks that line the Hudson River Valley in Putnam and Orange Counties. Here rolling green mountains produce a chlorophyll-fueled wonderland of unending forests extending in every direction, fringed along the water's edge with brackish marshes and narrow, sandy beaches. Trails penetrate the forests and climb up and over summits, leading to secreted lakes, misty cascades, the occasional cave or jutting overhang, and mercurial streams that appear in a rainy flash and vanish soon after. Granite ledges show off sweeping views of the lush landscape from on high, rewarding you with the verdant eye candy you came so far to see. These are the Hudson Highlands, protected in the park of the same name as well as in Harriman, Bear Mountain, Sterling Forest, Storm King, Fahnestock, and other state parks alongside the river.

Here you will find history as well as natural splendor. The remains of mining operations, the stone walls left behind by farmers and industrious landowners, the carriage roads enjoyed by the fabulously wealthy, and even the ruins of a once-grand estate all reveal themselves as you hike these trails. What you don't see is the plundered, denuded landscape left behind by aggressive lumber operations in the nineteenth century, stripping mature old-growth trees off these hillsides and leaving them to run with silt in spring rains and late winter snowmelt. It took the near ruination of this area to spark early environmentalists to act on the Hudson Highlands' behalf, and we have their restoration efforts to thank for the undulating emerald mountains we enjoy today.

Consider the hikes chosen for this section to be like dim sum on a Sunday morning, with one choice from each cart. When you've tried these, you're sure to want many more, so I urge you to discover what lies beyond each hill and past each new trailhead. The bounty you will find in these parks gets better with each step, and you will find yourself spending many weekends exploring the Highlands and discovering the favorite hikes that will bring you back again and again.

Find Canopus Lake at the end of the Three Lakes Trail in Clarence Fahnestock Memorial State Park.

8. LITTLE STONY POINT

WHY GO?

Add this hike on to any Hudson Highlands State Park adventure to see the sights from the Hudson River as well as the mountaintops.

THE RUNDOWN

Start: Little Stony Point Parking area on NY 9D in Cold Spring, Hudson Highlands State Park Preserve
Elevation gain: 137 feet
Distance: 0.7-mile loop
Difficulty: Easy
Hiking time: About 45 minutes
Seasons: Year-round
Schedule: Open daily, sunrise to sunset
Fees and permits: No fees and permits required
Trail contact: Hudson Highlands State Park Preserve, Route 9D, Cold Spring, NY 10516; (845) 225-7207; parks.ny.gov/parks/9/hunting.aspx
Dog-friendly: Dogs permitted on leash
Trail surface: Dirt and sand
Land status: New York state park preserve

Nearest town: Village of Cold Spring, New York
Other trail users: Hikers only
Maps: NatGeo TOPO! Map (USGS): West Point, NY; NatGeo Trails Illustrated Map #1508: Appalachian Trail, Delaware Water Gap to Schaghticoke Mountain; New York–New Jersey Trail Conference Trail Map #102: East Hudson Trails
Special considerations: Hunting is permitted in the Hudson Highlands in season, although not at Little Stony Point; archery and firearms hunting in designated areas for deer in fall and turkeys in spring. Take appropriate precautions (wear bright-colored clothing, especially orange) if you are visiting the rest of the park.

FINDING THE TRAILHEAD

From New York City, take NY 9A North from West 79th Street. In 1 mile, take the Saw Mill River Parkway north to NY 100/NY 9A North in Mount Pleasant. Take the NY 100 N/NY 9A N exit from the Taconic State Parkway. Continue on NY 9A North 34 miles to US 9 North. Take US 9 North to NY 403 in Philipstown then follow NY 403 North to NY 9D North in Cold Spring. Continue through Cold Spring to the Little Stony Point parking area on NY 9D North (on your left). **Metro North:** Cold Spring Station.

From the north, take I-84 East to NY 9D South in Philipstown. Turn right on NY 9D South and continue to the Little Stony Point parking area on NY 9D (on your left). The official street address is 3011 Route 9D, Cold Spring, NY.
Trailhead GPS: N41 25.590' / W73 57.944'

Stand on the bridge into Little Stony Point and watch Metro North trains pass under you.

WHAT TO SEE

It's easy to head straight for the highlands once you've found parking near Little Stony Point, which serves as the main parking area for hikes including the Cornish Estate Trail, Undercliff Trail, Washburn Mountain Trail, and Breakneck Ridge. But before you do (or once you've returned to your vehicle), take half an hour to visit Little Stony Point and see the surrounding mountains from the banks of the Hudson River.

I won't pretend that this is a major hiking adventure; there's no need to load up your backpack unless you plan to bring a picnic and savor the view over some bread and cheese. Little Stony Point gives you the opportunity to slow down and absorb a magnificent water's-edge view of peaks including Storm King and Crow's Nest without having to think about making your way back down from a summit or calculating the time it will take to return to your vehicle. In a couple thousand feet, you've reached the main attraction: expansive views of open water, sand, and green mountains, and the option of dipping your toes into the waters of the Hudson or sitting on a driftwood log and contemplating this reality.

Tucked away on this trail are some intriguing bonuses. A bridge takes you across the Metro-North train tracks, where you can watch the trains pass below your feet and get

From the beach at Little Stony Point, Storm King Mountain and Butter Hill rise across the river.

Caves offer an added bonus at Little Stony Point.

some nifty photos if you're quick. If you happen to arrive at low tide, you can walk out to a small island with a single tree on it—but remember to return from the island before the incoming tide cuts you off from shore. Best of all, on your way back from the beach, you can't miss the cave that appears on your left. This is a mine shaft, where quarry workers may have stored explosives when the mine was active. As the park doesn't know exactly

THE PERFECT PLACE FOR A WALLBOARD FACTORY?

Standing at Little Stony Point and gazing at the unparalleled view, it may seem impossible to believe that someone saw this as exactly the right spot to create an industrial site. That's what nearly happened in 1967, however, when the Georgia Pacific Company bought this land to build a wallboard factory.

When neighbors and environmentally conscious residents heard the news, they moved quickly to save the popular scenic spot from such a fate. The Hudson River Valley Commission and the State Council of Parks appealed to New York Governor Nelson Rockefeller, whose family had a history of preserving open space in the Hudson Valley and across the country. Rockefeller worked with Georgia Pacific to relocate the factory site to Verplanck, another peninsula farther down river, where considerable development had already taken place. Little Stony Point survived, and three years later the state added it to Hudson Highlands State Park.

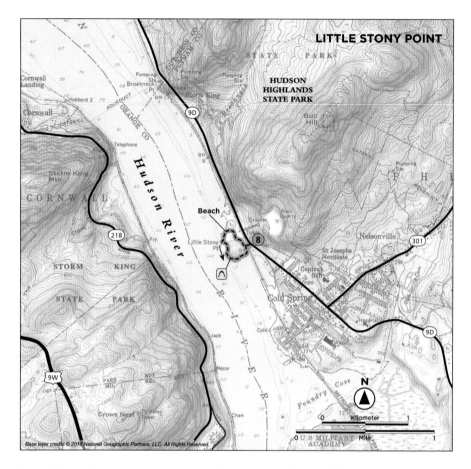

how this opening was used or what residue may have been left behind, please don't go inside.

Given that this cozy hideaway offers an unofficial beach, you may find your moment of solitude ending abruptly when families with lawn chairs, children, and dogs arrive to take advantage of the river access. Little Stony Point can be very popular on hot summer days, attracting boats as well as bathers (although swimming is illegal) and taking on the atmosphere of Jones Beach, with radios blasting away any hope of a wilderness experience (though amplified music is officially forbidden). You may be happier here on a cool day or even in winter. The view is just as remarkable whether it's January or July, so plan to enjoy some extra time taking in the sights whenever you arrive.

MILES AND DIRECTIONS

0.0 Start at the trailhead at the west end of the parking area. Go past the metal gate, cross the bridge over the railroad tracks, and turn right. You will see red blazes around the perimeter of the peninsula and green blazes that go to the river overlook. These directions roughly follow the red blazes.

0.1 At the intersection, go right. Bear left toward the river.

0.3 A sandy beach at the edge of the river provides fabulous views to the right, left, and straight ahead. Storm King is in front of you. Breakneck Ridge is to your right (north). Proceed as far up the beach as you can (west, to your left) until you reach the pile of rocks. Look left and you'll see a kiosk in the woods. Turn into the woods and continue on the trail just behind the kiosk. Turn right on the trail to continue along the water.

0.5 The main and waterside trails converge. In a short distance you'll find a mine shaft. The trail climbs briefly and then heads away from the river and back to the parking area.

0.7 Arrive back at the parking area.

9. HUDSON HIGHLANDS STATE PARK PRESERVE: CORNISH ESTATE– UNDERCLIFF TRAIL LOOP

WHY GO?

The lush emerald views from the top of this challenging trail remind you why you love Hudson Valley hiking.

THE RUNDOWN

Start: Little Stony Point Parking area on NY 9D in Beacon, Hudson Highlands State Park Preserve
Elevation gain: 1,100 feet
Distance: 4.4-mile loop
Difficulty: Strenuous
Hiking time: About 4 hours
Seasons: Year-round
Schedule: Open daily, sunrise to sunset
Fees and permits: No fees or permits required
Trail contact: Hudson Highlands State Park Preserve, Route 9D, Cold Spring, NY 10516; (845) 225-7207; parks.ny.gov/parks/9/
Dog-friendly: Dogs permitted on leash

Trail surface: Dirt, lots of loose rocks, large rock slabs
Land status: New York state park preserve
Nearest town: Cold Spring, New York
Other trail users: Trail runners
Maps: NatGeo TOPO! Map (USGS): West Point, NY; NatGeo Trails Illustrated Map #1508: Appalachian Trail, Delaware Water Gap to Schaghticoke Mountain; New York–New Jersey Trail Conference Trail Map #102: East Hudson Trails
Special considerations: Wear sturdy footwear with good ankle support. Consider a walking stick or ski poles to help with areas of loose cobbles and boulders.

FINDING THE TRAILHEAD

From New York City, take NY 9A North from West 79th Street. In 1 mile, take the Saw Mill River Parkway north to NY 100/NY 9A North in Mount Pleasant. Take the NY 100 N/NY 9A N exit from the Taconic State Parkway. Continue to follow NY 9A North 34 miles to US 9 North. Take US 9 North to NY 403 in Philipstown, and continue on NY 403 North to NY 9D North in Cold Spring. Continue through Cold Spring to the Little Stony Point parking area on NY 9D North (on your left). **Metro-North:** Cold Spring Station.

From the north, take I-84 east to NY 9D South in Philipstown. Turn right on NY 9D South and continue to the Little Stony Point parking area on NY 9D (on your right). **Trailhead GPS:** N41 25.590' / W73 57.944'

Explore the ruins of the Cornish estate before heading to the top of the Undercliff Trail.

WHAT TO SEE

If you've never ventured into Hudson Highlands State Park Preserve, consider this loop trail as an overview of the park and the many riches you will find here. The Cornish Estate Trail is an easy walk to the ruins of a once-majestic estate; the Undercliff Trail climbs to a combined scramble and rock-hop over a boulder-strewn trail corridor, finally rewarding you with sprawling views of the river and valley below; and the Washburn Trail features lots of cobbles that roll under your feet with each step. Bring your ski poles or walking stick and brace yourself for a demanding hiking experience—but one rewarded by satisfying panoramas once you reach the top.

Stretching about 16 miles along the east shore of the Hudson River in a series of detached land parcels, Hudson Highlands includes the Osborn Preserve, Bull Hill, Breakneck Ridge, Sugarloaf Mountain, the south summit of Mount Beacon, and Beacon Reservoir, as well as Bannerman Island and Denning Point. The park's 6,000-plus acres remain almost completely undeveloped, so while the trails are unusually well marked and easy to follow, that's just about all the obvious human intervention you will find here. Please remain on the trails—with the increased popularity of this preserve, it's imperative that hikers keep to the trails and help this wilderness stay pristine.

At this junction, the bridge leads to the Breakneck Ridge Trail. Keep following the Undercliff Trail to the right.

LOVE AMONG THE RUINS

I mentioned at the outset the ruins of the Cornish estate, the mansion and grounds once known as Northgate. Back in 1917, 56-year-old Edward J. Cornish married Selina Coe Bliss Carter (who was 67). The newlywed couple bought this 650-acre estate from diamond merchant Sigmund Stern, who had built it for himself and his family in the early 1900s. Here the Cornishes lived in comfort and created a sprawling country home with gardens, a swimming pool, a greenhouse, a barn that housed the family's prizewinning Jersey cows, and many other amenities, bringing in their friends for house parties and enjoying their decision to reject life in the city in their autumn years. Edward Cornish funded this pleasant life through his position as president of National Lead Company.

It seemed they would share this harmony until the end of their days—and they did, as they passed away in 1938 within two weeks of each other. Edward died at his desk at age 77; Selina passed away shortly thereafter at age 88. The mansion stood empty, the grounds went to seed, and eventually the dilapidated property was destroyed by fire in 1956 (though some reports say 1958). The ruins, while fascinating to examine, still retain an air of melancholy, the ravages of wind and weather having taken their toll on the remaining brickwork. Recently discovered photos of the estate in its heyday reveal that the mansion had a Tudor Revival design with shingle-style architecture. If you're a fan of mysterious places, make a stop here as you round the bend from the Cornish to the Undercliff Trail. (Please don't climb the ruins—save your scrambling for the trail.)

What you will witness with every step, however, are the Herculean efforts made by the state of New York and groups of concerned citizens to rescue and preserve this land after iron and copper mining, logging, and other industrial pursuits scraped the surrounding mountains nearly bare. Citizens formed an organization called the Hudson River Conservation Society to lead the charge against further industry incursion, working at the grassroots level (literally, in this case) to convince landowners to donate their holdings to the New York State Department of Environmental Conservation. Even though these efforts began back in the 1930s, it wasn't until the 1960s that the state made significant headway in turning land into parks. When Consolidated Edison proposed a hydroelectric power plant that would dominate Storm King Mountain, the state drew the proverbial line in the sand and redoubled its preservation efforts.

Major headway began when the Rockefeller family gave a deed of trust to the state for land purchases, allowing New York to acquire about 2,500 acres along the river and forever protect it from development. Another 1,033 acres came from landowner and conservation leader William Henry Osborn in 1974, and Scenic Hudson, now a powerful land trust, acquired other parcels to bring the park to its current shape and size.

Note: The Hudson Highlands have seen a recent surge in popularity, with people taking the train up from New York to the seasonal Breakneck Ridge stop and hiking through the park on a number of trails, completing their day by boarding the train at Cold Spring station at the other end of the park. This has made some of the trails particularly crowded

Rest and enjoy the view of Storm King Mountain (left) and Breakneck Ridge (right).

on weekends. If you crave solitude, visit this park on a weekday for the most satisfying experience. If you love seeing hundreds of people enjoying the Hudson Valley wilderness areas as much as you do, however, join the fun and come on a Saturday or Sunday. We hiked on a Saturday and thoroughly enjoyed the collective experience. Just please, please stay on the trails, and help the park maintain the beauty of this special place.

MILES AND DIRECTIONS

0.0 Start from the parking area at Little Stony Point, cross the road, and proceed to the well-marked trailhead. Follow the Cornish trail (blue markers).

0.3 The blue trail turns right on a paved road. (There's a gate to your left; don't go that way.)

0.8 At the Y junction, follow the directions on the sign and bear right for the Undercliff Trail. The ruins of the Cornish Estate is to your left—you may want to make a quick side trip for a closer look. In a moment, the pavement ends and the trail becomes crushed stone.

1.2 Here is a stone structure that looks like a well; it's more of the Cornish estate.

1.4 The trail splits. Go right on the blue trail.

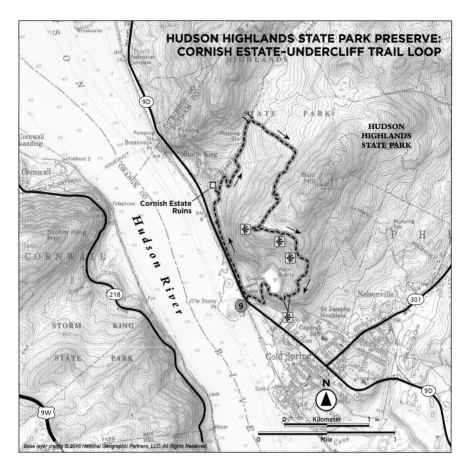

1.5 The red trail joins the blue trail from the left. Continue straight, now following the red trail along a stream. The trail is now strewn with rocks.

1.6 The green trail ends here on your left, at the stream crossing. Continue straight.

1.7 The bridge to your left is where the yellow (Undercliff) trail joins. Follow the yellow markers and blazes from here. Watch for arrows painted on rocks on the ground. There will be a lot of rocks. In a moment the yellow trail turns right. From here it's a climb over a rocky trail with boulders that get larger as you go.

2.4 After an uphill stretch you reach a high point. It's not the highest point. Continue straight on the yellow trail.

2.9 Reach the first great viewpoint. There are big rock slabs here on which you can sit and enjoy the view east of the Hudson River.

3.0 Reach the second excellent viewpoint.

3.2 The white (Washburn) trail joins here. This is your route down. Turn right on the white trail.

3.3 Come to another nice viewpoint.

3.8 At this viewpoint, you can see how far down you've already come (about 700 feet). In about 0.1 mile there's a last view of the Hudson before the final descent.

4.0 When you come out of the woods, turn left on the white trail. The big rocks are behind you; the rest of the trail is cobbles and sandy soil.

4.4 Arrive back at the trailhead. The parking area is across the road.

10. BREAKNECK RIDGE

WHY GO?

Scramble up rock faces, work your way along ledges, and find your way to some stunning views on the toughest hike in the Hudson River Valley.

THE RUNDOWN

Start: Parking area on NY 9D north of Cold Spring, north of the tunnel
Elevation gain: 1,442 feet
Distance: 3.6-mile loop
Difficulty: Strenuous
Hiking time: About 4 hours
Seasons: Spring through fall
Schedule: Open daily, dawn to dusk
Fees and permits: No fees or permits required
Trail contact: Hudson Highlands State Park Preserve, Route 9D, Cold Spring, NY 10516; (845) 225-7207; parks.ny.gov/parks/9/hunting.aspx
Dog-friendly: Dogs permitted on leash but not recommended
Trail surface: Dirt, rock slabs, rock formations
Land status: New York state park
Nearest town: Cold Spring, New York
Other trail users: Hikers only
Maps: NatGeo TOPO! Map (USGS): West Point, NY; NatGeo Trails

Illustrated Map #1508: Appalachian Trail, Delaware Water Gap to Schaghticoke Mountain; New York–New Jersey Trail Conference Trail Map #102: East Hudson Trails
Special considerations: In fall 2017, a major improvement project was scheduled to begin on Route 9D at the Breakneck Ridge trailhead as part of the Hudson Highlands Fjord Trail construction project. During the construction, the Breakneck trailhead was expected to close temporarily. Check hudsonfjordtrail.org for updates on trail progress and trailhead closings before your hike.

This trail involves some serious rock scrambling. It's not recommended for young children, for parents with baby carriers either in front or behind, or for dogs (unless you can carry them up very large rocks).

FINDING THE TRAILHEAD

From the village of Cold Spring, head north on NY 9D for about 1 mile. At the far end of the tunnel, turn left into the large parking area. If there aren't any spots there, head north about 200 yards to a larger lot on the left. **Metro-North:** Cold Spring; Breakneck Ridge stop on weekends in season (check schedule at http://web.mta.info/mnr/html/planning/schedules/).
Trailhead GPS: N41 26.756' / W73 58.750'

WHAT TO SEE

No book about hiking the lower Hudson Valley would be complete without the area's signature hike to Breakneck Ridge. Its rocky cliffs, visible from miles away, came into being during quarrying operations in the 1850s, but this fact does not detract from the imposing figure they strike on the Hudson Highlands skyline.

With its daunting 1,200-foot elevation change in less than a mile of hiking, Breakneck is widely considered the most difficult day hike in the valley, yet literally thousands of people undertake it on any weekend from April through November, until snow makes the trail impassable.

Not everyone completes this hike, and I must admit to my readers that I did not. The scrambles up tall rock ledges were more than my aging knees could handle—I simply don't bend that way these days. Breakneck Ridge must be part of this book, however, so I asked a much younger leading expert to serve as a guest writer about this remarkable hike. I'm delighted (and relieved) to introduce Michael C. Todd, whose "Hike the Hudson Valley" website at hikethehudsonvalley.com has been a terrific resource for me in choosing hikes to include in this book.

Breakneck Ridge may be the toughest hike in the Hudson Valley. MIKE TODD

Here's what Mike has to say about the experience; the Miles and Directions below are from his hike:

Mike: Until recently, I didn't understand why Breakneck Ridge was such a wildly popular hike. It had been many years since I'd climbed it, and my most vivid memory from Breakneck was our friends hoisting their Black Lab over some rocks that were too steep for their poor pooch to climb. Nearby Bull Hill offers similar views without Breakneck's crazy steepness. Why would anyone want to climb an elevator shaft when they could just take the stairs instead?

In preparing this write-up, I gave Breakneck another shot, taking half a day off work to meet my buddy Rob, who hopped the train from Grand Central up to Cold Spring, about a mile south of the trailhead. (For New York City hikers, there's also a Breakneck Ridge MTA stop right across the street from the trailhead, with a limited weekend-only schedule of six trains daily in each direction.)

Shorter than many area hikes, the trail climbs to the top of a man-made ridge.
MIKE TODD

After hiking the loop up Breakneck again, I can't understand why I ever thought this place was anything short of spectacular. With multiple cliff overlooks and ever-expanding views the entire way up, this hike is not to be missed.

It is extremely difficult, though, and I'd be very hesitant to recommend this hike for small children. I've done most of the hikes in Hike the Hudson Valley with a baby on my back, but I'd never attempt that here. I didn't see any other dogs there that day, but a fellow hiker assured me that she sees dogs here all the time. There were several spots where my pooch, Memphis, needed a boost, and I honestly don't see how a dog would get over some of those spots without being picked up and placed on top of the rocks.

The point I'm trying to make: This hike is steep.

It is also gorgeous and unforgettable. If you have a chance to pay a visit to Breakneck Ridge, don't pass it up. And if you don't have a chance, you should probably make one anyway.

MILES AND DIRECTIONS

0.0 Start from the parking area and head to the northern side of the tunnel. Climb up and over the tunnel that runs over NY 9D, following the white trail markers. Keep climbing up and up and up.

The view from the top includes a head-on look at Storm King.
MIKE TODD

0.5 After what feels like quite a climb (because it is), you'll come to a flagpole with a great overlook. Across the river is Storm King Mountain. To your right is Pollepel Island, with Bannerman's Castle perched on the side, and the Newburgh-Beacon Bridge beyond. Keep following the white markers up. There are a few spots where you can choose steeper or less steep options, marked with an X pointing left and right.

1.0 Keep climbing, and eventually this mountain will run out of bluffs to throw at you. Really, it will. When it feels like you're at the top and you can't see any more bluffs in front of you, you're probably there. At the top, above a couple of nice little pine trees, enjoy the view and munch a granola bar or two. The

IT ISN'T NATURAL
Randi here. The funny thing about Breakneck Ridge is that it's not a natural formation. These cliffs are the result of quarrying that took place in the nineteenth century, long before the Hudson Highlands became the focus of environmentalists' attention. The stone harvested from this mountain served in the construction of the military academy at West Point, the Brooklyn Bridge, and even as the steps of the Capitol in Albany, New York. You can thank industry, not Mother Nature, for the indomitable rock faces, sheer cliffs, and vertical bluffs you'll encounter on this hike.

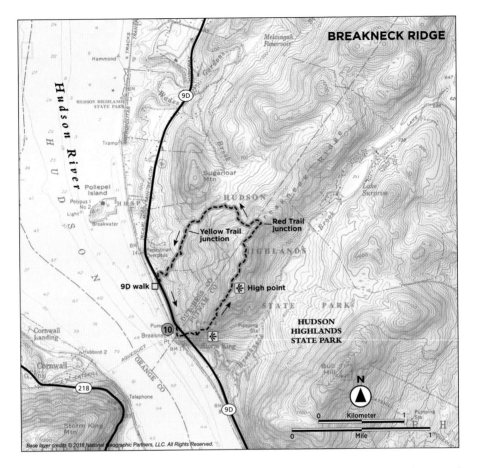

BREAKNECK RIDGE

Red Trail junction

Yellow Trail junction

9D walk

High point

HUDSON HIGHLANDS STATE PARK

Base layer credits © 2018 National Geographic Partners, LLC. All Rights Reserved.

next 3.0 miles on the loop will fly by in comparison. Keep heading straight on the white trail; ignore the yellow trail as it departs to your right.

1.6 After you pass one last small summit and a small wetland on your right, the turnoff to the Breakneck Bypass (red markers) is very tough to miss. When you see it, take a left. Follow the red trail down a much more gradual descent through the woods, with occasional northerly views of Sugarloaf Mountain and the river.

2.5 In about 30 to 60 minutes, depending on how leisurely you're strolling, the red trail dead-ends into the Wilkinson Memorial Trail, marked in yellow. Turn left on the yellow trail and keep following it downhill.

3.0 The yellow trail continues its gradual descent for 15 minutes or so, ending abruptly and dumping you unceremoniously onto NY 9D. This can be a very busy road. Turn left onto NY 9D and walk carefully on the well-worn path beside it.

3.6 Carefully cross the street to get back to your car. Boom! You did it. Congratulations on knocking out one of the toughest hikes in the area.

11. CLARENCE FAHNESTOCK MEMORIAL STATE PARK: THREE LAKES TRAIL

WHY GO?

Find some real solitude among the ponds, lakes, gentle forested hills, and back roads of this tranquil park.

THE RUNDOWN

Start: Parking area on Dennytown Road that also serves the Catfish Loop and the Appalachian Trail. This is the second parking area if you're driving south on Dennytown Road from NY 301.
Elevation gain: 257 feet
Distance: 3.8-mile shuttle (7.6 miles out and back)
Difficulty: Moderate
Hiking time: About 3 hours (6 hours out and back)
Seasons: Spring through fall
Schedule: Open daily, dawn to dusk
Fees and permits: No fees or permits required
Trail contact: Fahnestock State Park, 1498 Route 301, Carmel, NY 10512; (845) 225-7207; parks.ny.gov/parks/133/
Dog-friendly: Dogs permitted on leash

Trail surface: Dirt, woodland detritus, rocks, large rock formations
Land status: New York state park
Nearest town: Carmel, New York
Other trail users: Anglers at ponds
Maps: NatGeo TOPO! Map (USGS): Oscawana Lake, NY; NatGeo Trails Illustrated Map #1508: Appalachian Trail, Delaware Water Gap to Schaghticoke Mountain; New York–New Jersey Trail Conference Trail Map #103: East Hudson Trails; trail map available online at parks.ny.gov/parks/attachments/ClarenceFahnestockTrailMap.pdf
Special considerations: Wear boots with ankle support. Be aware that black bears have been sighted in the vicinity of the park; know what to do if you encounter a bear.

FINDING THE TRAILHEAD

From the Taconic State Parkway, take the exit for NY 301. Drive west (south) on NY 301 to the parking area at Canopus Lake, directly across from the Three Lakes Trailhead (blue markers; GPS: N41 27.294' / W73 50.025'). Park one car here, and leave the parking area heading northeast on NY 301. Continue to Denny-town Road; turn left. Follow Dennytown Road to the second parking area on your left (you will see a small stone building and a trailhead kiosk; GPS: N41 25.266' / W73 52.099'). Park your second car here and begin your hike at the Three Lakes Trailhead.
Trailhead GPS: N41 25.266' / W73 52.099'

WHAT TO SEE

Just east of Hudson Highlands State Park Preserve lies a park more than twice the size of the Highlands, a protected area large enough to allow visitors to find quiet places and solitude without running into hordes of eager hikers. Clarence Fahnestock Memorial State Park began as a 2,400-acre wilderness donated to New York State by Dr. Ernest Fahnestock in 1929, creating a memorial to his brother Clarence that would endure for many generations. Additions over the ensuing century expanded the park to include an area designated for winter activities like snow-tubing and cross-country skiing, lakes that provide satisfying fishing and ice fishing, a bridle path for equestrians, and turkey and deer hunting in season.

The Three Lakes Trail winds along the shores of John Allen Pond and Hidden Lake, coming to an end at the parking area at Canopus Lake. Along the way you'll find the remains of several mines—areas where workers blasted deep into solid rock and left the indentations in the hillsides to wear away over time. Journalists James Kelly and Michael Turton of the *Highlands Current* looked into the origins of these mines in 2013 and discovered a complex history. In the eighteenth and nineteenth centuries, industrial operations made use of the Reading Prong, a vein of iron ore that runs underground

John Allen Pond welcomes anglers and paddlers as well as hikers.

You can see plenty of signs of beaver activity around Hidden Lake.

from western Connecticut to Reading, Pennsylvania. Here they mined pure black magnetite, a particularly highly valued variety of iron ore, in some of the oldest mines in the area. Activity ratcheted up significantly during the Civil War as immigrants from Ireland, England, and Scotland worked the mines day and night to provide ore to the West Point Foundry, where each ton of ore was refined into 1,000 pounds of pig iron. This iron in turn became guns and ammunition, making these mines key advantages in the Union's war effort.

The Three Lakes Trail follows this vein of precious minerals, though the mines have long since closed and the towns that sprang up around them were dismantled when mining in the area came to an end. Imagine, however, a thriving hamlet here in the vicinity of the Dennytown Road parking area, with a school, housing for miners and their families, a Methodist church, stores, and mining company buildings instead of the open fields and forests we see today.

So what happened to the mines? With the opening of transcontinental commerce made possible by railroads, foundries turned to the more accessible mines in Minnesota and Michigan for their ore. The mines at Dennytown closed in 1874. For a short time in the 1880s, Thomas Edison attempted to use some of the area's mines to test his magnetic ore separator, but when this invention did not work well enough to market it, he abandoned the project. The mines closed for good after that, and Clarence Fahnestock purchased the land from the mining company in 1915 with an eye toward preserving the open space.

Today you can meander through this wild land and see beaver activity along John Allen Pond, deer peeking at you through the oak forest, colonies of chipmunks rustling through last season's leaves, a garter snake or two crossing your path, and maybe even a fox watching you from the other side of a lake. We spotted bear scat on the trail but did not see the animals themselves. That being said, take the necessary precautions (see the list of bear encounter techniques at the beginning of this book). You are sure to hear red-eyed vireo, common yellowthroat, wood thrush, yellow warbler, American robin, blue jay, northern cardinal, and white-crowned sparrow in the shady woods. This park is a special place.

MILES AND DIRECTIONS

0.0 Start at the trailhead in the northeast corner of the parking area. Follow the blue markers.

A carpet of ferns greets hikers between Hidden and Canopus Lakes.

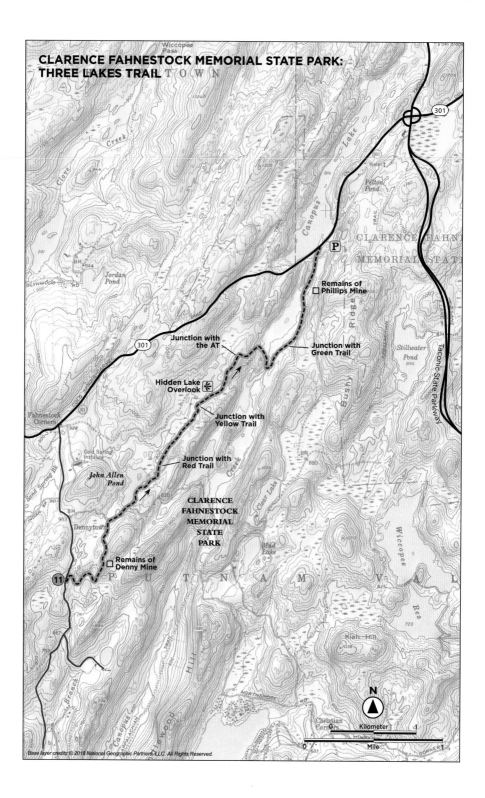

CLARENCE FAHNESTOCK MEMORIAL STATE PARK: THREE LAKES TRAIL

301

Remains of Phillips Mine

Junction with the AT

Junction with Green Trail

Hidden Lake Overlook

Junction with Yellow Trail

Junction with Red Trail

301

John Allen Pond

CLARENCE FAHNESTOCK MEMORIAL STATE PARK

Remains of Denny Mine

11

N

Kilometer

Mile

0.3 The trail goes up through a rocky area. You may need to do some scrambling.

0.4 The remains of Denny Mine are visible to your right. After this, the trail begins to descend.

0.6 You're in a valley. Continue straight.

0.8 John Allen Pond comes into view on your left. There's a path down to the water here if you'd like a closer look.

0.9 Turn left at the side trail (following blue markers). Cross a stream on rocks— look left to see a waterfall. There's a lot of beaver activity visible here.

1.4 The red trail goes right. Continue straight.

1.9 The yellow trail goes left. Take the trail that bears right (this is still the blue trail).

2.1 Reach the Hidden Lake overlook.

2.4 At the junction with Appalachian Trail (white blazes), continue straight.

2.6 There's a marsh on your right.

2.8 Cross a creek on big slabs of rock.

3.1 The green trail joins here. Turn left and continue to follow the blue trail.

3.5 Phillip Mine remains are on either side of the trail.

3.8 The trail ends at NY 301 and the parking area.

12. BEAR MOUNTAIN STATE PARK: APPALACHIAN TRAIL TO THE SUMMIT

WHY GO?

Hike this meticulously maintained trail to the summit of the Hudson Highlands' crown jewel.

THE RUNDOWN

Start: Parking area across from the Appalachian Trail's northern trailhead on Seven Lakes Drive in Bear Mountain State Park. (**Note:** The AT crosses Seven Lakes Drive in two places—one in Harriman State Park, and one in Bear Mountain State Park. Be sure that you're at the right one by using the GPS coordinates below.)

Elevation gain: 747 feet

Distance: 3.2 miles out and back

Difficulty: Moderate

Hiking time: About 2.5 hours

Seasons: Spring through fall

Schedule: Open daily, dawn to dusk

Fees and permits: No fees or permits required

Trail contact: Bear Mountain State Park, 3006 Seven Lakes Dr., Bear Mountain, NY 10911; (845) 786-2701; parks.ny.gov/parks/13/details.aspx

Dog-friendly: Dogs permitted on leash

Trail surface: Dirt, rock, sandy soil, stone steps

Land status: New York state park

Nearest town: Highland Falls, New York

Other trail users: Hikers only

Maps: NatGeo TOPO! Map (USGS): Peekskill, NY; NatGeo Trails Illustrated Map #756: Harriman, Bear Mountain, Sterling Forest State Parks; trail map available online at parks.ny.gov/parks/attachments/BearMountainTrailMap.pdf

Special considerations: This trail includes some narrow ledges and many stone steps.

FINDING THE TRAILHEAD

From the Palisades Parkway, take exit 19 for Bear Mountain State Park and Perkins Memorial Drive. Head east on Seven Lakes Drive to the first right turn you see; this is an unlabeled parking area. Park here, cross Seven Lakes Drive, and walk east about 100 feet to the Appalachian Trail trailhead (white blazes).
Trailhead GPS: N41 18.239' / W74 00.803'

WHAT TO SEE

Bear Mountain! The name alone invites admiration and longing from hikers throughout the Hudson Valley region, whether they have climbed it and come home to tell the tale

Thank the New York-New Jersey Trail Conference and their affiliates for the meticulously maintained Bear Mountain Trail

ALL THIS, AND A ZOO TOO

Bear Mountain State Park not only offers one of the area's most pleasing trails to some of the greatest views in the Hudson Valley, but it even has a zoo. The Trailside Museum and Zoo provides homes to birds and mammals that have been permanently injured or orphaned and would not be able to survive in the wild, as well as a fascinating collection of native reptiles and amphibians. Here in the Trailside Museum and Zoo, you can see a timber rattlesnake, spotted salamander, spring peeper, or box turtle in the Reptile and Amphibian House, or visit with a red fox, an opossum, a porcupine, or an eastern coyote—even a black bear. The raptor center in Trailside's upper area regularly shelters red-tailed and rough-legged hawks, bald eagle, barred owl, long-earned owl, turkey vulture, and other birds of prey. It's worth driving into the park after your hike to see animals up close that may have hidden in the vast wilderness while you were on the trail.

or dream they will hike it one day. At just 1,283 feet, Bear Mountain is far from the highest in the area—Catskill mountains just to the north tower over it by 2,000 feet or more—but its magnificent views of the surrounding Hudson Highlands and the Catskills in the distance make it a favorite with day hikers, Appalachian Trail thru-hikers, and folks who drive to the top just to enjoy a picnic and watch the sunset.

Yes, you can drive your car to the summit, but the trek up this small section of the Appalachian Trail is such a pleasure that you'll really miss a great hike if you opt to take your car. You can thank the work of the New York–New Jersey Trail Conference in partnership with the Appalachian Trail Conservancy, the National Park Service, the Palisades

The Appalachian Trail route up the mountain alternates between stone steps and level stretches.

At the top of Bear Mountain, rest and admire the view from a unique bench.

Interstate Park Commission, and the New York State Office of Parks, Recreation and Historic Preservation for creating the stone steps that take you up much of the mountain to the most amazing viewpoints. The NYNJTC's volunteers have been at work on this mountain for more than a decade, building the fully accessible walkway at the top of the mountain, relocating parts of the trail that were damaged by erosion, and creating what *Backpacker* magazine dubbed a "masterpiece trail."

This hike up the West Mountain portion of the trail is the shorter route along the AT, though it provides enough elevation change to get your blood pumping with great vigor. Stone steps, the occasional cleverly placed handrail, and fresh, easily spotted blazes make this an unusually pleasant trail to navigate. Best of all, you'll receive major rewards as you reach the ledges toward the top of the mountain—sublime, panoramic views that are worth this effort and more.

At the top, take a moment to visit the Perkins Memorial Tower, built to honor George W. Perkins, the founder and first president of the Palisades Interstate Park Commission (PIPC). We can thank Perkins for the salvation of the Palisades cliffs, which had been targeted by the construction industry to harvest basalt, a key building material. Perkins also fought to keep the state from moving Sing Sing Correctional Facility to Bear Mountain, a battle he eventually won in 1910, even though construction had begun on the prison building. In addition, he arranged for the gift of $1 million from the Harriman family (as well as a total of $1.5 million from John D. Rockefeller and J. P. Morgan) to create Harriman State Park.

MILES AND DIRECTIONS

0.0 Start from the parking area, cross Seven Lakes Road, and head east to the trailhead.

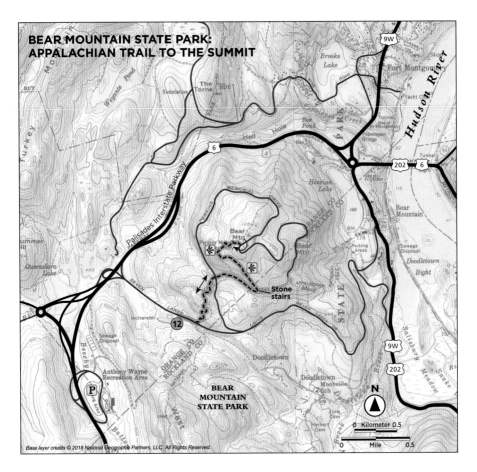

0.1 Turn left on the Appalachian Trail (white blazes). Make sure you're heading north on the trail.

0.2 Stone steps. There's a handrail embedded in the rock here to help you up.

0.6 Cross Perkins Memorial Road and continue following the white blazes. The trail levels out for a while.

1.0 A long stone stairway begins here.

1.1 Here's the first big viewpoint.

1.4 Reach another great viewpoint.

1.5 You can see blue blazes here. This is a nice shortcut to the top of the mountain. Go ahead and follow the blue trail here.

1.6 Reach the Bear Mountain Hikes trail map at the top of the trail. The summit (1,355 feet) is just ahead. Head back the way you came.

3.2 Arrive back at the trailhead.

13. STORM KING MOUNTAIN AND BUTTER HILL

📷

WHY GO?

Hike up a Hudson Valley icon to some of the area's most sumptuous views of the Highlands, the Catskills, and the ribbon of river below.

THE RUNDOWN

Start: Storm King parking area, directly off US 9W north of West Point and south of Cornwall-on-Hudson

Elevation gain: 516 feet

Distance: 2.3-mile loop

Difficulty: Strenuous

Hiking time: About 2.5 hours

Seasons: Spring through fall

Schedule: Open daily, dawn to dusk

Fees and permits: No fees or permits required

Trail contact: Storm King State Park, Mountain Road, Cornwall-on-Hudson, NY 12520; (845) 786-2701; parks.ny .gov/parks/152/details.aspx

Dog-friendly: Dogs permitted on leash

Trail surface: Dirt, rock, some large rock slabs, some scrambling

Land status: New York state park

Nearest town: Cornwall-on-Hudson, New York

Other trail users: Trail runners

Maps: NatGeo TOPO! Map (USGS): West Point, NY; NatGeo Trails Illustrated Map #1508: Appalachian Trail, Delaware Water Gap to Schaghticoke Mountain; New York–New Jersey Trail Conference #113: West Hudson Trails

FINDING THE TRAILHEAD

On the Palisades Interstate Parkway, drive to the northern end of the parkway at Bear Mountain Circle. Take the exit for US 9W and continue about 8 miles to the second Storm King State Park parking area—watch for the historical marker about Freedom Road. Turn sharply right into the parking area.
Trailhead GPS: N41 25.390' / W74 00.096'

WHAT TO SEE

One of the most popular hikes in the Lower Hudson Valley, the route up Storm King Mountain by way of Butter Hill earns its reputation by providing one sparkling viewpoint after another for the entire length of this challenging trail. A clear day at the top can reveal the Catskill Mountains rolling beyond the Shawangunks, the Hudson River's silvery ribbon extending all the way to New York City, and unsurpassed views of the mountains nearby, including Bull Hill, Mount Beacon, Crow's Nest, and Schunemunk.

The views from the top of Storm King Mountain and Butter Hill are more than worth the effort.

It's commonly believed that Storm King is the highest of the Hudson Valley mountains, but that honor actually belongs to Schunemunk Mountain at 1,663 feet. This doesn't diminish the power of the view from the top of either Storm King or Butter Hill, and this hike takes you to both, leading up Butter Hill before you reach Storm King. So you may not be at the top of the area's highest peak, but you get a bonus summit to enjoy and more fantastic views to admire.

As mountain hikes go in this region, Storm King is not the hardest—though you will do some scrambling up areas of exposed granite, and there are plenty of rocks and roots in the path to keep an eye on. If you've had some experience hiking in the area, you'll find this route to be no more difficult than Anthony's Nose, and probably easier than many hikes in the Hudson Highlands. It's the many viewpoints that make this such a legendary climb, not the difficulty; the views make the many rock-strewn passages, ankle-turning boulders, and oh-my-god moments entirely worthwhile.

Standing atop either of these mountains and gazing out over the expansive landscape, it's hard to believe that people once thought it would be a good idea to build a pump storage hydroelectric plant here, running transmission lines across the Hudson River and blasting away a large area of the mountain where it reaches the river. That was the plan back in 1963, and it became the catalyst for an extraordinary effort on the part of concerned citizens to stop Consolidated Edison from realizing its goal. The Federal Power Commission granted ConEd a license to begin construction, but residents of the Hudson Valley had no interest in seeing the project move forward because of its impact on both the area's scenic beauty and the health of the river. They formed the Scenic Hudson Preservation Conference (today known as Scenic Hudson) and took on the Federal Power Commission in the US courts—even though the FPC had denied that

Looking north from the Storm King summit

an environmental activist group could bring such an action against them. The appeals court ruled in favor of Scenic Hudson, however, giving legal standing to an environmental group for the first time in the nation's history. Even so, it took fifteen years to stop the project, with Scenic Hudson and other organizations fighting it on every front until ConEd withdrew its plan to build a plant. The effort remains a landmark in the development of environmental law, which hardly existed before the citizens of the Hudson Valley stepped forward to protect their river and its scenic treasures.

MILES AND DIRECTIONS

0.0   Start in the parking area and walk to the western end until you see three orange blazes and three white blazes on a tree to your right. This is the trailhead; you will follow the orange blazes. (The white blazes are the Bypass Loop, your return trail.)

0.2   Here is your first viewpoint, at the top of a big rock field. There's a nice view of the river to your left, and of US 9W below. In a moment you'll come to the ruins of Spy Rock House, with three stone chimneys and the remains of a foundation. Here Dr. Edward L. Partridge, a devoted advocate for the preservation of the Hudson Highlands in the early 1900s, made his summer home. From here the trail levels off, descends a bit, then starts up another rocky area.

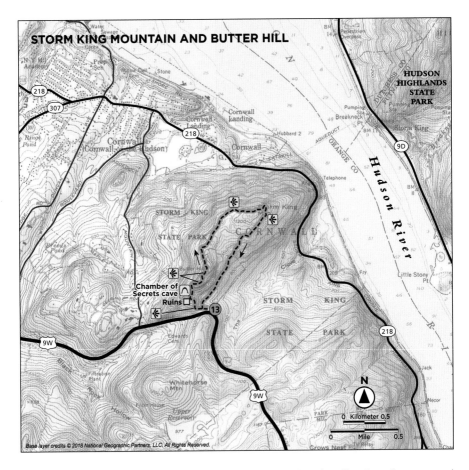

0.3 There's a cave to your right with graffiti that labels it the "Chamber of Secrets." (Please don't see this as permission to tag the rocks. It's illegal to deface state property, and it's just a rotten thing to do.) From here, the climb looks harder than it actually is. You'll find fairly easy footing as you go up this rock field.

0.4 After a scramble, arrive at a 270-degree view just before the summit of Butter Hill. From here you can see US 9W and Crow's Nest Mountain to the south and the Hudson River to the east.

0.5 The orange trail ends at the yellow trail, also known as the Stillman Trail. The trail has two blazes: yellow and turquoise. Turn right on this trail. In a moment you'll come to an open ledge with a terrific view. Note Mount Beacon to the north (with the towers on it), Bull Hill to the east, and Crow's Nest Mountain to the south. The Butter Hill summit is just ahead.

0.7 Reach a junction with the blue and red trail (Bluebird Trail). Go right and continue following the yellow trail. In a moment you'll see the blue blazes for the Howell Trail. Keep following the yellow trail. The trail soon starts to climb again.

1.0 Here's a ledge with a great view. This is not the Storm King summit, but it's worth a stop.

1.2 Arrive at the Storm King summit. Stop to enjoy the view from the ledge.

1.4 This ledge shows you more of the view to the north.

1.7 To your left there's a ledge with a great view to the south. To your right the white trail (Bypass Trail) begins. Follow the white trail.

1.8 The blue (Howell) trail joins the Bypass Trail here. Continue straight on the white trail.

2.3 Arrive back at the parking area.

14. HARRIMAN STATE PARK: PINE SWAMP MOUNTAIN

WHY GO?

Clear mountain lakes, forest-covered peaks, rocky outcroppings, and a summit with a spectacular view—it's all worth the extra effort Harriman demands.

THE RUNDOWN

Start: Parking lot for Lake Skannatati on Seven Lakes Drive
Elevation gain: 1,021 feet
Distance: 2.7-mile loop
Difficulty: Strenuous
Hiking time: About 2 hours
Seasons: Spring through fall
Schedule: Open daily, dawn to dusk
Fees and permits: No fees or permits required
Trail contact: Palisades Interstate Park Commission, Bear Mountain, NY 10911; (845) 786-2701; nysparks.state .ny.us/parks/145/details.aspx
Dog-friendly: Dogs permitted on leash

Trail surface: Dirt and rocks
Land status: Harriman State Park
Nearest town: Highland Falls, New York
Other trail users: Trail runners, mountain bikers
Maps: NatGeo TOPO! Map (USGS): Sloatsburg, NY; NatGeo Trails Illustrated Map #756: Harriman, Bear Mountain, Sterling Forest State Parks; New York–New Jersey Trail Conference #119: Harriman Bear Mountain Trails
Special considerations: Boots with ankle support are a must in this park.

FINDING THE TRAILHEAD

From I-87, take exit 15A (Sloatsburg). Turn left at the bottom of the ramp onto NY 17 North, and drive through Sloatsburg. Turn right at the first traffic light after the village onto Seven Lakes Drive. Continue on Seven Lakes Drive for 8 miles to the parking area for Lake Skannatati, on the left side of the road. (The parking area is 0.7 mile after the Kanawauke Circle.)
Trailhead GPS: N41 14.426' / W74 06.153'

WHAT TO SEE

What does the quintessential downstate New York hike look like? Look no further than Harriman State Park, where this loop—a relatively easy hike compared to the rest of the park—takes you through areas of mixed forest, huge boulders, and exposed faces of granite and metamorphic gneiss. The payoff comes at the top of Pine Swamp Mountain,

Follow the Long Path (aqua blazes) to begin the hike to Pine Swamp Mountain.

a low peak by Adirondack standards but with a sweeping view of the surrounding Hudson Highlands. You'll be glad you braved the vigorous ascent when you arrive at the top.

Choosing one hike in Harriman is an almost ridiculous proposition—like choosing one tiny meatball from an enormous banquet table—but this hike provides an overview of many of the park's most appealing features. Here you'll have the pleasure of admiring Harriman's intriguing geology, with large areas of visible rock faces and narrow trails between big formations. You'll have the opportunity to admire one of the park's shimmering lakes at the beginning of the hike, and you can poke through areas disturbed more than a century ago by industrial activity—long since reclaimed by second-growth woods and aggressive vegetation. Finally, there's the view from the top of Pine Swamp Mountain, not the highest peak in Harriman's collection but a fairly easily accessible one with a short scramble to an immensely satisfying panorama. I hope this taste of the park will encourage you to try some of the longer and more challenging hikes listed in the "Bonus Hikes" section of this book.

You may expect old-growth forest here, but most of the trees here are second-growth, replanted after decades of iron mining stripped this area bare before and after the Civil War. The mines' furnaces required copious amounts of charcoal made from firewood, turning the forest into a continuous raw fuel source for iron ore processing. Mining stopped when Pennsylvania coal and Minnesota iron began to overshadow the Highlands' iron production at the turn of the twentieth century. That's when the Harriman family presented the State of New York with 10,000 acres of their private land adjacent to an existing park as well as a $1 million donation to endow Bear Mountain, turning this area into an outdoor paradise for hikers, campers, boaters, and many others.

The remains of decades of iron mining are visible here.

The trail is clear and easy to follow as you approach the summit.

While this hike takes you through the remains of some of these mines, they are not easy to spot, in part because the land has recovered so strongly from the mining days. Today the land appears as natural as it may have before the mines, the forests broken only by peaceful blue lakes and silver-gray rock faces jutting through the thriving understory.

The first part of this hike follows the Long Path, a footpath from Altamont in the Albany area all the way to the George Washington Bridge in Fort Lee, New Jersey. Originally a project of the Mohawk Valley Hiking Club, this 347-mile trail crosses the Shawangunk and Catskill Mountains, winding through salt marshes at its southern end and climbing to 4,000 feet in the Catskills' boreal forests. It's only recently that the "parakeet aqua" blaze color has been used from one end of the trail to the other, but wherever you see this shade, you'll know you're on the Long Path.

MILES AND DIRECTIONS

0.0 Start at the Lake Skannatati parking area and begin following the aqua blazes at the northwest corner of the lot. You'll see white blazes with a red inverted triangle here as well; this is your return trail to the lot at the end of your hike. Almost immediately, another path goes right; bear left along the edge of the lake and follow the aqua blazes.

0.2 Turn right on the aqua-blazed path. (Another path goes left here.)

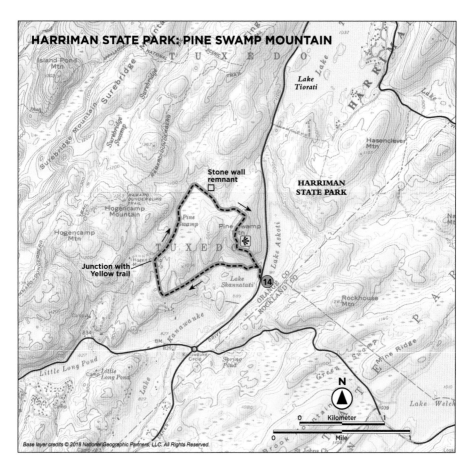

HARRIMAN STATE PARK: PINE SWAMP MOUNTAIN

0.8   Cross a stream on large boulders. Begin a short ascent.

1.1   The yellow trail goes left and right here. Turn right on the yellow trail and begin following a dirt road.

1.5   You're in a young hemlock woods. The pond to your right is the center of Pine Swamp. Look for remnants of Pine Swamp Mine ahead.

1.7   Reenter the woods here. Three yellow blazes on a tree signal the end of the yellow trail. Turn right and follow the white blazes with a red inverted triangle in the center. This is the Arden-Surebridge Trail (A-SB). Cross a stream on rocks (this may be a rushing torrent in spring). In about 10 steps there's a box canyon to your left; explore if you wish. Continue on the A-SB when you're ready.

1.8   There's a cascade to your left; it may be dry in summer. In about 400 feet you'll see a remnant of a stone wall. This is all that remains of the area in which miners lived from the 1830s to the 1880s. The trail ascends steeply for a short stretch here and then begins an up-and-down section on a rockier path.

1.9   Begin a gradual but challenging 0.5-mile ascent to the top of Pine Swamp Mountain.

2.4   You've reached the summit of Pine Swamp Mountain at 1,165 feet. The view is obscured at this spot; continue to follow the trail to your left (south) for a better vantage point.

2.5   Here's the view you came to see. Skannatati and Askoti Lakes lie in front of you, and the forest-covered Catskill Mountains extend to the west, north, and south. You can see Seven Lakes Road below, the only road that traverses this vista. When you're ready, follow the A-SB trail blazes downward to your left. The descent begins as a bit of a scramble over large boulders, but soon it becomes an easy, shady descent through the woods.

2.7   Arrive back at the parking area.

15. CONSTITUTION MARSH AUDUBON CENTER AND SANCTUARY

WHY GO?

Take an intimate look at a tidal marsh from the inside, surrounded by head-high vegetation, gently flowing water, and the songs of marsh-loving birds.

THE RUNDOWN

Start: Parking area at the intersection of Warren Landing and Indian Brook Roads.
Elevation gain: 222 feet
Distance: 1.1-mile lollipop
Difficulty: Moderate
Hiking time: About 1 hour
Seasons: Year-round; best Apr–Nov
Schedule: Trails open during daylight hours; may close in winter due to icy conditions
Fees and permits: No fees or permits required
Trail contact: Constitution Marsh Audubon Center and Sanctuary, 127 Warren Landing Rd., Garrison, NY 10524 (physical address); PO Box 174, Cold Spring, NY 10516 (mailing address); (845) 265-2601; http://constitutionmarsh.audubon.org
Dog-friendly: Dogs not permitted
Trail surface: Dirt path and boardwalk

Land status: Audubon center and sanctuary
Nearest town: Cold Spring, New York
Other trail users: Hikers only
Maps: NatGeo TOPO! Map (USGS): West Point, NY; NatGeo Trails Illustrated Map #1508: Appalachian Trail, Delaware Water Gap to Schaghticoke Mountain; trail map available online at constitutionmarsh.audubon.org/sites/g/files/amh661/f/22_hikes_in_philipstown.pdf
Special considerations: Please visit http://constitutionmarsh.audubon.org for important information about a safe and enjoyable visit. Sunscreen is critical; insect repellent is not. Parking is very limited. Your best bet is to arrive early on a weekend day or visit on a weekday.

FINDING THE TRAILHEAD

The sanctuary is on the east side of the Hudson River at 127 Warren Landing Rd. in Garrison. From I-87, take exit 17 toward I-84/Newburgh/Stewart Airport. Merge onto I-84 East and continue to the NY 9D exit. Turn right at the end of the ramp and follow 9D south to Indian Brook Road. Take a slight right here and continue to the parking area at the intersection of Indian Brook and Warren Landing Roads.
Trailhead GPS: N41 24.090' / W73 56.268'

The boardwalk at Constitution Marsh extends well into the open wetland.

WHAT TO SEE

Not many rivers in the United States have the close connection to ocean tides that we find here at the Hudson River. According to local legend, Native Americans called the river *Mahicanituck*, or "waters that never stand still," and they learned to use the ebb and flow of the tidal current to navigate in small boats. The river hosts five tidal marshes that behave much like the salt marshes found in ocean ecosystems. Constitution Marsh is one of these, and its unique ecosystem has earned it designations as a Significant Coastal Fish and Wildlife Habitat, a New York State Bird Conservation Area, and an Audubon Important Bird Area.

It's one thing to stand on the edge of a marsh and peer into it to see what's going on—it's quite another to walk right into the tall grasses and reeds and become part of the action. The boardwalk at Constitution Marsh gives you exactly this opportunity, providing a sturdy, remarkably unobtrusive route into the heart of this tidal marsh.

Your hike begins with a fairly quick descent from the parking area down a dirt road, bringing you to the visitor center with its interpretive displays and restrooms (open Tues through Sun, 9 a.m. to 5 p.m.). Listen for Louisiana waterthrush here, one of the sanctuary's specialty birds. From here follow the blue trail into the woods and up a challenging incline to a rewarding view of the marsh and the Hudson River beyond.

A quick descent brings you to the boardwalk, where the fun really begins. This gorgeous cattail marsh resonates with marsh wrens' chatter, punctuated by calls of the occasional common yellowthroat or red-winged blackbird. Song sparrows pop up to the tops of the tall grasses, while Virginia rails skulk quietly at the edge of the reeds. A belted kingfisher may land on the boardwalk railing to check you out. Muskrat lodges—piles of sticks and mud—may be visible at the base of the cattails. Watch for these animals and for fish in the calm waters as you pause at the boardwalk's many viewing areas.

You may also spot some of the dominant species of invasive plants, especially purple loosestrife and common reed growing tall in the marsh, European water chestnut blanketing the water's surface, and mute swans—a particularly striking bird that has made itself a nuisance with its prolific breeding

Only a few marshes along the Hudson River support cattails, an important source of shelter for birds, animals, and insects.

The boardwalk provides great birding during the spring and fall migrations

throughout waterways in the northeastern United States. Audubon staff members have worked hard to reduce common reed throughout the sanctuary, using aggressive measures including covering wide areas of this invasive species with sheets of black plastic. You may glimpse some of this as you view the marsh; it's a necessary and highly effective procedure that will improve the health of the marsh over time.

Looking across the marsh, you can enjoy a spectacular view of the Hudson Highlands. Storm King Mountain and Mount Taurus are easily visible, as is the United States Military Academy at West Point.

You'll return the way you came, through the woods and down the rocky paths. While this may not be the largest wildlife sanctuary in this book, it's a satisfying walk, with more nature packed into a condensed area than many trails can show you over several miles.

MILES AND DIRECTIONS

0.0 Start from the parking area and walk downhill to the southwest until you reach the visitor center. The trailhead is past the visitor center on the edge of the woods.

0.3 Follow the blue diamond-shaped markers. The trail begins as a mowed grass path, but once you cross a small bridge, it changes to a dirt path through the woods. At the T intersection, bear left on the blue trail. Bear right at the next intersection.

0.4 The trail turns right and goes up a set of rock steps. Soon you reach an overlook, where you can see the marsh through the maple and pine trees. Continue up the stone walkway and steps to the bench at the top of the hill.

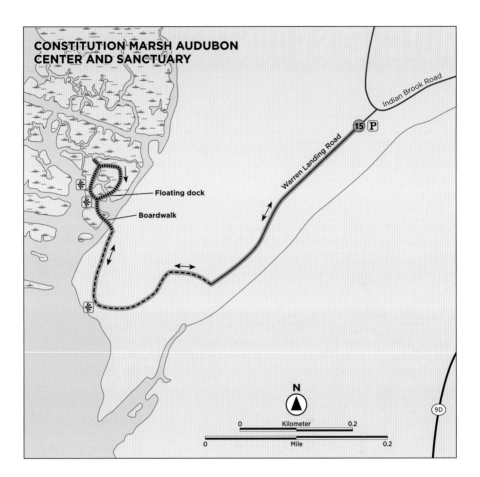

The view of the marsh and the Hudson River is worth a pause to catch your breath. From here the trail descends to the boardwalk.

0.5 The boardwalk begins. Enter the tidal marsh, where high tide occurs every 12.5 hours. The tide brings ocean fish up into the river, and they stop here to lay their eggs. If you're here in summer, watch for young fish in the open waters. The boardwalk forms a loop, with three viewing platforms and benches along its route.

0.6 You've completed the boardwalk loop. Return the way you came, on the straight section of boardwalk and over the hill to the visitor center.

0.8 Arrive at the visitor center. Turn northeast and walk up the road to the parking area.

1.1 Arrive back at the parking area.

DUTCHESS COUNTY

Scenic wonders meet American history in Dutchess County, the residential choice of the twentieth century's wealthiest industrialists. It's easy to see why so many mansions sprang up in this area along the river, with its wild forests, high vistas, green hills, and hidden lakes and ponds. Here these captains of capitalism could truly have it all, balancing natural surroundings with proximity to New York City and the work that made their lifestyle possible.

Here Franklin Roosevelt and his wife, Eleanor, made homes together and separately as they worked to govern the country and direct it out of the Great Depression. Their next-door neighbors, the Vanderbilt family, built railroads that widened commerce from a local to a national scope. Samuel Morse worked with others to invent the telegraph and bring it to market, uniting the country with a communication network faster than anything seen that time. These were just a few of the many titans who built opulent

In a county steeped in history, Top Cottage provides an intimate perspective of Franklin Roosevelt.

homes here in the cradle of the Hudson River Valley, choosing to spend some of their most productive and most relaxed times in these pleasant surroundings.

Today environmentally minded people have come together to protect Dutchess County's green spaces, laying claim to gems like Winnakee Nature Preserve and Dover Stone Church as well as the vast tracts of forest along the river. Here you can discover special places like Tivoli Bays Wildlife Management Area and Thompson Pond, and you can hike the entire length of the town of Hyde Park to explore three of its national parks. Even with the variety of hikes selected for this section, however, there are dozens of others in the area that may delight you. Choose from the samples presented here, and let them lead you to new adventures in this delightful county.

16. TIVOLI BAYS WILDLIFE MANAGEMENT AREA

WHY GO?

A bluff-top view of a freshwater tidal marsh awaits you at the end of this trail, while the route through wild, open meadows and dense woodlands reveals habitat for a wide assortment of birds, butterflies, and small furry creatures.

THE RUNDOWN

Start: Parking area on NY 9G between Cruger Island Road and Kidd Lane in Annandale-on-Hudson

Elevation gain: 278 feet

Distance: 2.6-mile lollipop

Difficulty: Easy

Hiking time: About 1.5 hours

Seasons: Spring through fall

Schedule: Open daily, dawn to dusk

Fees and permits: No fees or permits required

Trail contact: NYS Department of Environmental Conservation, Norrie Point Environmental Center, PO Box 315, Staatsburg, NY 12580; (845) 758-7010; dec.ny.gov

Dog-friendly: Dogs permitted on leash

Trail surface: Dirt and mowed grass path

Land status: Hudson River National Estuarine Research Reserve

Nearest town: Annandale-on-Hudson, New York

Other trail users: Trail runners, bicyclists; cross-country skiers in season

Maps: NatGeo TOPO! Map (USGS): Clermont, NY; trail map available online at dec.ny.gov/docs/remediation_hudson_pdf/tivoli.pdf

Special considerations: Hunting is permitted here in season; take precautions (wear bright-colored clothing, especially orange) if you hike here during hunting season. Watch out for poison ivy along trails. Railroad tracks in and near the preserve are active with high-speed trains; do not walk on or play near the tracks.

FINDING THE TRAILHEAD

From I-87, take exit 19 toward Kingston and the Kingston-Rhinecliff Bridge. At the traffic circle, take the first exit onto NY 28 North. Merge onto US 209 North and continue on US 209 for 3.8 miles. Stay on this road as it becomes NY 199, and cross the Kingston-Rhinecliff Bridge. Turn left at the junction with NY 9G. Continue 4.5 miles to the parking area for Tivoli Bays Wildlife Management Area, on your left.

Trailhead GPS: N42 02.167' / W73 53.741'

WHAT TO SEE

It may surprise you that the Hudson River is affected by Atlantic Ocean tides, but the ebb and flow that reach the river's mouth in Long Island Sound have an influence upriver all the way to the Federal Dam in Troy. The complex ecosystem is known as the Hudson River Estuary, and one of the best places to see how its tides create a freshwater marsh is at the end of this trail.

Here the Tivoli Bays are miraculously safe from development, thanks to the work of the Hudson River National Estuarine Research Reserve, which uses this area as a field research center. The state's Department of Environmental Conservation oversees protection of the land we cross on this hike, for the good of the wildlife that thrives in this area.

And what exciting wildlife it is! Blue-winged warblers call from vine-covered trees in the middle of meadows; pileated woodpeckers announce their presence as they excavate new cavities in dead trees; red admiral butterflies dart from one blossom to the next. Vireos, warblers, thrushes, jays, and orioles pause here on their way to breeding grounds farther north, or remain to repopulate their species right here, where abundant natural food is within easy reach of nest sites. A trail of bluebird boxes erupts with tiny peeps as busy eastern bluebirds fly off to forage for food and return to their nestlings with full bills.

Healthy vegetation blankets the fields with green in spring.

Snapping turtles, the granddads of aquatic life at Tivoli Bays, often bask in the sun.

Sunset over Tivoli Bays is not to be missed.

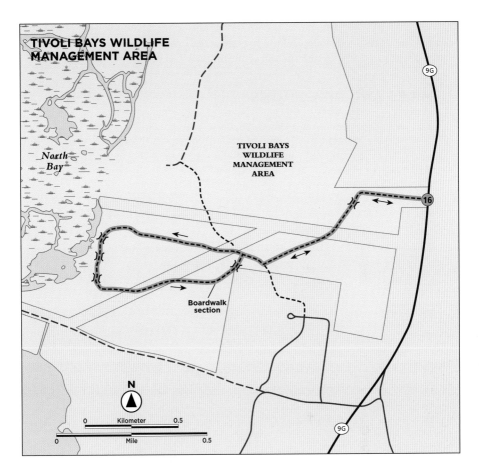

Marsh wrens fill the air with their chatter as you reach the overlook, and careful observers may spot a Virginia rail or least bittern among the cattails. In the woods, chipmunks and squirrels vie for the best food and places to store it, while signs at the parking areas note that black bears occasionally make appearances here.

As a freshwater tidal marsh surrounded by undeveloped forest, Tivoli Bays WMA is unique on the Hudson River. This makes it prime habitat for shorebirds, ducks, large wading birds, and other waterfowl at any time of year. If you arrive here at low tide, you may glimpse shorebirds poking their bills into the mud at the South Bay. Dabbling ducks, including the prevalent American black duck, are likely during the spring and fall migrations, and least bitterns are seen here regularly.

Your hike begins by following the Overlook Trail (red markers) to an excellent view of Tivoli Bays and then turns onto the North Bay Trail (blue) until it reaches the Hogback Trail (yellow) for a short ascent into a drier portion of the woods. The route finally rejoins the Overlook Trail and follows it back to the parking area. You may want to make this hike close to sunset so you can take in the sight from the Overlook Trail—or stop at either of the boat launches, particularly the one at the end of Cruger Island Road on the Bard College campus, to watch the sun set from water level.

MILES AND DIRECTIONS

0.0   Start at the parking lot on Route 9G. There's only one trailhead from here, leading into the woods. Follow the red plastic markers that say "Trail" or "Foot Trail." Cross through thick vegetation, then through a more-open area.

0.2   A path goes off right; continue straight. In about 50 steps the red trail turns left. In a short while, cross a small bridge over a stream.

0.4   There's no bridge here, but there may be water in the stream during snowmelt season or after heavy rains. Cross on rocks. In a few steps, cross another stream on rocks.

0.5   The trail leaves the woods and enters an open meadow. Continue across.

0.6   Merge here with a crushed-stone path and turn right.

0.7   A trail with yellow markers goes left here. Pass it and turn left on the next trail, which has red markers.

1.2   Reenter the forest and continue to the overlook point. From here you have a view through the trees, where you can see Tivoli Bays and the many grassy islands created by the tide's rise and fall. When you're ready, turn left on the blue trail. Begin a fairly easy descent.

1.3   At the bridge, turn left. Cross two more bridges.

1.5   The Hogback Trail (yellow markers) goes left here. Turn left and begin a gradual ascent.

1.9   Cross a section of boardwalk. Then cross a bridge and emerge in the meadow.

2.0   When you see the red trail markers, turn right and begin your return on the red trail. Follow this back to the parking area.

2.6   Arrive back at the parking lot.

17. MOUNT BEACON PARK

WHY GO?

Get ready for some uphill switchbacks and rocky terrain, and reap the reward of dazzling viewpoints at the summit.

THE RUNDOWN

Start: Parking area at 788 Wolcott Ave. in Beacon, New York (Parking is limited here; there's additional parking at the Fishkill Ridge parking area at 35 Sunnyside Rd.)
Elevation gain: 1,022 feet
Distance: 2.0 miles out and back
Difficulty: Strenuous
Hiking time: About 2 hours
Seasons: Year-round
Schedule: Open daily, dawn to dusk
Fees and permits: No fees or permits required; available for special events and group outings: scenichudson.org/whatyoucando/visitourparks/specialeventpermits
Trail contact: Scenic Hudson, One Civic Center Plaza, Suite 200, Poughkeepsie, NY 12601; (845)

473-4440; www.scenichudson.org/parks/mountbeacon; e-mail: info@scenichudson.org
Dog-friendly: Dogs permitted on 6-foot leash (Please clean up and carry out any waste.)
Trail surface: Gravel, metal stairs, dirt and rock, some stretches of loose rock and large rock slabs
Land status: Scenic Hudson Land Trust
Nearest town: Beacon, New York
Other trail users: Trail runners, mountain bikers; snowshoers in season
Maps: NatGeo TOPO! Map (USGS): West Point, NY; trail map available online at scenichudson.org/sites/default/files/Mt.Beacon.webmap.png

FINDING THE TRAILHEAD

From the south, take NY 9A to the Palisades Interstate Parkway North. Drive 43 miles to the exit for US 202/US 6 East in Highlands. At the traffic circle, take the second exit and continue on US 202/US 6 East. Bear left on NY 9D North, and continue 14 miles through Beacon to the Mount Beacon parking area at 788 Wolcott Ave. From the north, take I-87 South to exit 11, for NY 9D South in Fishkill. Turn right onto NY 9D South and continue through Beacon on NY 9D to the Mount Beacon parking area at 788 Wolcott Ave.
Trailhead GPS: N41 29.614' / W73 57.600'

WHAT TO SEE

Don't be fooled by the easy metal staircase at the beginning of this hike. The 154 steps do you the courtesy of carrying you to the base of the first switchback up Mount Beacon, but from there the trail extends nearly a mile along the zigzagging route as you make your way to the top. This side of Mount Beacon is the slightly less strenuous way to reach

Don't be fooled by the stairway—the hike to the top of Mount Beacon is not easy.

Switchbacks help make the trail to the top a little less strenuous.

the summit. If you're a climbing animal and this trail isn't challenging enough for you, take the one through the Hudson Highlands that traverses Breakneck Ridge on its way to Mount Beacon. That should do it.

The staircase is more than a courtesy here; it follows the route of the Beacon Incline Railway, the remains of which you can examine closely at the summit. Known as the world's steepest railway of its type when it opened in 1902, the railway served as a major tourist attraction and brought tens of thousands of eager patrons to a viewing platform with one of the most panoramic views of the Hudson River in the region. A hotel at the summit—constructed on the foundation you will see here—provided sightseers with meals, dancing, and overnight accommodations as they watched the sun set over the river and the Catskills. The 2,200-foot railway ran up and down the mountain until 1978, when repeated fires, debt, and other challenges forced the incline to close. As if all that wasn't bad enough, one last fire swept through the entire dormant railway system in 1983, leaving the structure and its operation completely unsalvageable. Today the Beacon Incline Railway Restoration Society is exploring ways to bring this historic transportation system back to life on the mountain.

Long before it provided views to tourists, however, Mount Beacon served a military purpose. If you explore a bit at the top, you will find a monument to the people who used the mountain's height to send messages to patriots fighting the British forces during the Revolutionary War. Here American soldiers waited and watched the river to see if the British were moving into the area from the north in an attempt to take the Hudson River, a key strategic resource for moving men and supplies. If the British came from the north, the soldiers would light a signal fire as a beacon—giving the mountain its name. The British came from the south instead of the north and took part of the river,

The fascinating ruins of the Beacon Incline Railway remain at the top of the mountain

but American defense strategies kept them from holding it. The monument here recalls some of these moments that shaped American history.

Today the venerable Scenic Hudson owns this side of the mountain, purchased over the course of three years in the 1990s. This parcel connects seamlessly to the 1,900 acres Scenic Hudson already owned on Fishkill Ridge, protecting a swath of land adjacent to Hudson Highlands State Park Preserve and the green spaces to the south. In 2015 Scenic Hudson transferred more than 2,100 acres on Mount Beacon and Fishkill Ridge to New York State and incorporated it into Hudson Highlands State Park.

MILES AND DIRECTIONS

- **0.0** Start from the trailhead and walk up the gravel path to the staircase.
- **0.2** Staircase. Walk up nine flights (about 154 steps).
- **0.4** Reach a junction with the beginning of the yellow trail. Continue on the red trail, around the corner of this switchback.
- **0.6** An unmarked trail goes left here. Continue on the red trail.
- **0.8** Another junction with an unmarked trail. Bear right on the red trail.

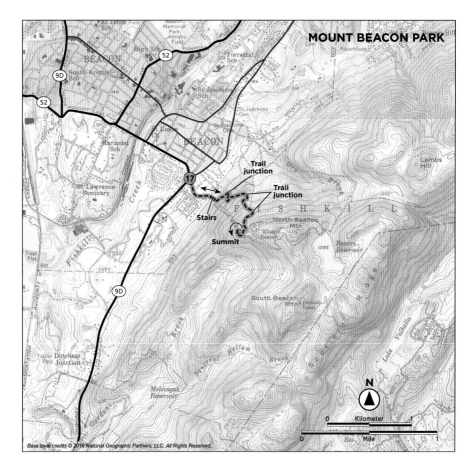

1.0 Reach the summit. When you're ready, return the way you came.

2.0 Arrive back at the parking area.

18. THOMPSON POND

WHY GO?

Circle a 15,000-year-old glacial kettle lake and discover a hidden wetland at the base of Stissing Mountain.

THE RUNDOWN

Start: Thompson Pond preserve entrance and parking area
Elevation gain: 40 feet
Distance: 2.6-mile loop
Difficulty: Easy
Hiking time: About 1.5 hours
Seasons: Year-round
Schedule: Open daily, dawn to dusk
Fees and permits: No fees or permits required
Trail contact: The Nature Conservancy, 195 New Karner Rd., Suite 200, Albany, NY 12205; (518) 690-7850; nature.org
Dog-friendly: Dogs not permitted
Trail surface: Dirt paths, some boardwalk

Land status: The Nature Conservancy preserve
Nearest town: Pine Plains, New York
Other trail users: Birders; cross-country skiers in season
Maps: NatGeo TOPO! Map (USGS): Pine Plains, NY; trail map available online at nature.org/ourinitiatives/regions/northamerica/unitedstates/newyork/places-preserves/thompsonpond.pdf
Special considerations: Insect repellent is a must. Guard against ticks by wearing long pants and tucking them into your socks. There is no boating on the lake.

FINDING THE TRAILHEAD

From the Taconic Parkway, take the exit for NY 199 and travel east on NY 199 to NY 82. Follow NY 82 South to Pine Plains and turn right on Lake Road. Continue 1.6 miles to the parking area and preserve entrance, on the left side of the road.
Trailhead GPS: N41 58.052' / W73 40.913'

WHAT TO SEE

Back when North America was beginning to warm up toward the end of the last ice age (about 15,000 years ago), a massive chunk of glacial ice scooped out a depression in an area west of today's Pine Plains. As the ice chunk melted, it filled the depression and created a sizable body of water. Time and erosion have divided this single body into Twin Island Lake, Stissing Pond, and Thompson Pond. The Nature Conservancy protects Thompson Pond, providing recreational access to this unusual kettle pond and its abundant plant and animal life.

A well-groomed trail leads around Thompson Pond.

A National Natural Landmark, the 530-acre Thompson Pond preserve has more claims to fame than its glacial origin. It contains a wetland that is calcareous, having a high concentration of calcium carbonate because of the limestone in its soil. This means the pond

LEGENDS, LORE, AND THE REVOLUTIONARY WAR

"I have long been intrigued with the story of Muggins Cave," wrote essayist Lois R. Palmatier of the Little Nine Partners Historical Society in 1969, "but hesitate to add it here because I have been unable to verify it." She goes on to tell it, however, so it's something to mull over as you enjoy your visit to Thompson Pond.

The story goes that the Muggins family, loyalists to British rule, took cover in a cave somewhere around Thompson Pond and Stissing Mountain—and stayed there for the entire Revolutionary War. They survived by only lighting their cooking fire at night when the mists forming over the lake hid their smoke, and we can only guess how they withstood the New York winters throughout the five years of the Revolution.

Nearly two centuries later, Professor Lyman Henry Hoysradt explored the area where the cave might have been and discovered what he believed to be the location. Here are the directions he shared with Palmatier: "Proceed down the old wood road as far as it goes, ending at the foot of a high rocky ledge. This appears to be a part of the mountain, but it is really an outcrop lying parallel to, but at some distance from it. If you go around the south end of this ridge, you will find a secluded glen with a stream coming from a spring on the mountain. This would make an ideal hideaway."

I haven't tried it myself, but if you do go exploring, please let me know what you find.

The trail leads up to the edge of several pond inlets.

Dame's rocket and other wildflowers bloom here throughout spring and summer.

and adjacent swamp can support wildlife and plants not found in many other wetlands. The plants you see here may seem strange and exotic, especially along the boardwalk through the swamp. Look for pipewort, marsh St. John's-wort, and unusual ferns and wildflowers. In all, 387 plant species thrive in this preserve alongside 27 mammal species.

If you're a birder, Thompson Pond is a special delight. Migratory waterfowl make this pond a stopover point as they make their way up and down the Atlantic Flyway. Virginia rails and soras live within the cattail community; listen for a sound like two rocks clacking together to find a rail at dawn or dusk. Red-tailed hawks nest nearby; watch for the many plumage variations worn by recently fledged hawks (but always with the russet-colored tail). Eagles, turkey vultures, and other hawks frequent the sky over the preserve, and warblers come through in May; many species stay in the area to nest and breed. In all, if you frequent this remarkable place, you might see as many as 162 different bird species over the course of a year.

Your hike follows the yellow-blazed trail all the way around the pond, through forests of maple, hemlock, hickory, and ash; along cattail marshes; past open farm fields and a cattle pasture; and through areas where wildflowers crowd the understory. With its fairly remote location and widely diverse habitats, this hike truly brings you into the wilderness for a much-needed break from civilized life.

If you're looking for a challenging hike after you complete this one, Stissing Mountain to the north (owned by the Friends of Stissing Tower and very visible from the pond) offers a 1.9-mile loop with a 926-foot elevation change. At the top of the mountain, you'll find a 90-foot fire tower (about 30 feet taller than other towers in the region) that you can climb to experience sweeping views of the Taconic Mountains and the Hudson Valley—if you don't mind scaling a delicate structure that sways in the wind. The hatch at the top remains open year-round, so you'll have a fairly solid resting place once you've conquered all those stairs.

MILES AND DIRECTIONS

0.0   Start at the roadside parking area. The trail begins due south of the road. Follow the diamond-shaped green markers with yellow arrows—this is the yellow trail.

0.3   Stop at the kiosk to check out the trail map. Make a quick detour by taking the blue trail (green markers with blue arrows) to your left for a view of the lake. Follow the blue trail around until it reconnects with the yellow trail.

0.5   Turn left as you rejoin the yellow trail. Now the trail is marked with yellow blazes on the trees as well as the plastic markers.

0.6   At this intersection, the blue trail goes right and the yellow goes left. Bear left on the yellow trail. The lake becomes more visible through the trees to your left.

0.7   A stone bench here marks a nice viewpoint.

0.8   Here's a second bench with a welcome view of the lake. From here the trail descends for a short stretch. You may see considerable evidence of beaver

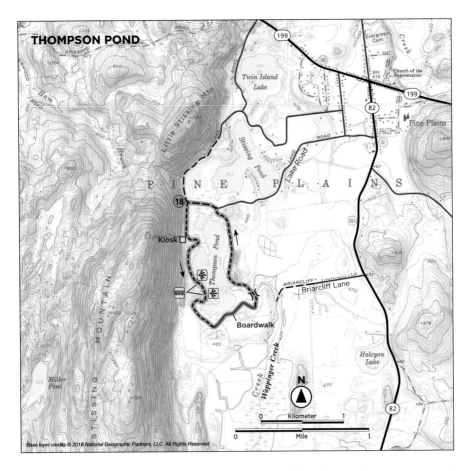

THOMPSON POND

activity here. Marsh wrens, yellow warblers, warbling vireos, and swamp sparrows all sing in the marsh along the pond.

1.0 The yellow trail goes left and the blue goes right. Go left and continue on the yellow trail. Be careful not to trip into the barbed wire fence on your right. The land beyond is a private farm.

1.2 Descend a set of steps to a narrow boardwalk over the swamp. This is the most fascinating section of the hike, with the feeling of a jungle or a tropical rain forest. Trees are covered with vines, plants have extra-large leaves, tree limbs overhang the trail, and tall grasses obscure the view on either side.

1.3 The boardwalk ends. Continue through an area of dense vegetation, with a bog to your left and rolling farmland to your right. This area can be muddy; there are some lengths of two-plank boardwalk to get you through the wettest portions.

1.6 Do you hear mooing? The farmer's dairy barn comes into view on your right. The last length of boardwalk ends here. In a moment the vegetation parts and you have a clear view of the pond. Tree islands grow here, with grasses at their bases and roots exposed above the water. You may see wild iris here in spring.

1.7 Cross a bridge. This is a good spot to stop and look at the tree-island area. You'll see lily pads here too, which bloom in midsummer. Reenter the woods.

2.1 A hunting field appears on the right after the woods. Continue straight. Ahead, the grassy areas fill with dame's rocket's purple and lavender flowers in spring and other wildflowers throughout summer. Berry vines here produces raspberries in July.

2.4 The trail ends at the road. Turn left to walk back to your car; be sure to stop and enjoy the view of the pond as you go.

2.6 Arrive back at the parking area.

19. DOVER STONE CHURCH

WHY GO?
An exquisite little trail leads to a cathedral-ceilinged cave with its own interior waterfall.

THE RUNDOWN

Start: Corner of NY 22 and Stone Church Lane in Dover Plains
Elevation gain: 59 feet
Distance: 1.0 mile out and back
Difficulty: Easy
Hiking time: About 45 minutes
Seasons: Year-round
Schedule: Open daily, dawn to dusk
Fees and permits: No fees or permits required
Trail contact: Friends of the Dover Stone Church, Dover Plains, NY 12522, and Town of Dover; (845) 832-6111; townofdoverny.us or facebook.com/groups/DoverStoneChurch/
Dog-friendly: Dogs permitted on leash; waste station bags and receptacle on-site

Trail surface: Crushed stone, rock slabs along stream
Land status: Town of Dover in partnership with the Dutchess Land Conservancy and the Friends of Dover Stone Church
Nearest town: Dover Plains, New York
Other trail users: Hikers only
Maps: NatGeo TOPO! Map (USGS): Pine Plains, NY; trail map available online at nynjtc.org/print/8813
Special considerations: The Stone Church Brook flows through the cave. Consider your ability to withstand the current before you step into the water. Current may be very strong following heavy rainfall.

FINDING THE TRAILHEAD
From the north, take NY 22 South to Dover Plains. The trailhead is at the corner of NY 22 and Stone Church Lane, across from Dover Elementary School.
From the south, take NY 22 North to Dover Plains, and follow directions above.
From the west, take NY 44 East and continue onto NY 343 East in Millbrook. Continue on NY 343 for 8 miles to the junction of NY 22 South in Dover Plains. Turn right onto NY 22 and see directions above.
Parking: Parking is available at Dover Elementary School after 3 p.m. or on weekends and holidays; the Tabor-Wing House south of the elementary school (3128 Route 22); or Freshco 22 Restaurant and Deli, at the intersection of NY 22 and Mill Street. Do not park at the gravel entrance to the trail; this is on private property and may only be used for pedestrian access.
Trailhead GPS: N41 44.383' / W73 34.842'

WHAT TO SEE
Where there's a cave, there's a legend, and Dover Stone Church has one of its own.

A lane of granite steps leads
down into the preserve.

Small waterfalls are particularly picturesque after a rain.

In the 1630s the Pequot grand sachem (chief) Sassacus used this cave on the Stone Church Brook as a hideout to escape English soldiers hunting for him. The English were only one of this chief's worries, however. The Pequots dominated the Mohegans, another tribe in the New London, Connecticut, area, led by sachem Uncas. The Mohegans joined forces with the English to rebel against Pequot rule, a conflict history records as the Pequot War—and one that Sassacus lost rather spectacularly. He fled the area—though some sources say he died here—and sought protection farther northwest with the Iroquois Mohawks, but they saw Sassacus as nothing more than a bargaining chip in their own relationship with the English. Some accounts say the Mohawks killed Sassacus, cut off his head and hands, and sent them to the English in Connecticut Colony as a peace offering. Others contend that he was captured and killed in the Danbury, Connecticut, area.

Happily, nothing else quite so dramatic took place in the history of Dover Stone Church, a particularly magical little place in Dover Plains that New York State had the good sense to list in its Open Space Plan as a site worthy of preservation. Privately owned until 2002, these 58.5 acres were purchased by the Town of Dover when they came up for sale with the help of the Dutchess Land Conservancy and the Friends of Dover Stone Church, a grassroots community group formed to preserve the site. Together they restored the maple tree–lined right-of-way, added granite stairways and a footbridge, and later opened three additional nature trails on land secured through purchase and conservation easements.

Your hike dips into the valley down cement stairs; follows the brook along a path created from wide, flat rocks; and reaches the Dover Stone Church in about 0.5 mile. When you see the cave opening, you will understand how it got its name. Arched like the roof of a cathedral, it glows from the inside because of openings in its ceiling that allow sunlight to provide an ethereal glow. Here you have the option of entering the cave if the brook is shallow on the day of your visit; if snowmelt or a recent rainstorm have turned the brook into a rushing stream, this is not the day to wade into the cave.

MILES AND DIRECTIONS

0.0   Start at the trailhead and take the crushed stone path to the stairs.

0.1   There are forty-one stairs down. At the bottom, cross an open meadow on a path lined with maturing maple trees.

0.2   Take the short staircase (eleven steps) up to the path. A creek comes into view on your left.

The brook leads directly to the stone church cave.

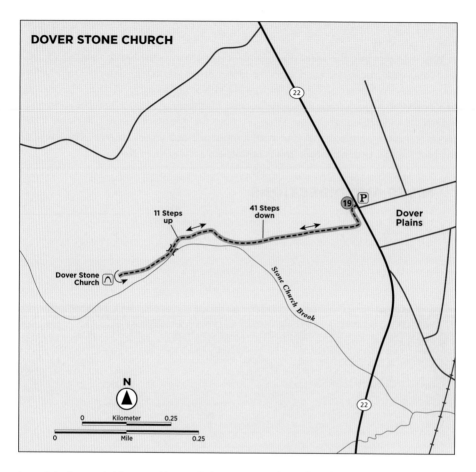

0.4 Cross a bridge over the creek. In a moment the trailheads for the red, yellow, and blue trails come into view. These trails all go left; you continue straight. The path becomes slabs of rock that hug the creek.

0.5 You've reached the cave known as the stone church. If the brook and water-fall are rushing, don't enter the water. If not, a creek walk will take you into the stone church to see the natural "pulpit" and the other fascinating rock formations inside. When you are ready, return the way you came.

1.0 Arrive back at the trailhead.

20. **LOCUST GROVE**

WHY GO?
Walk in the footsteps of the man who helped make the telegraph an international communications system.

THE RUNDOWN

Start: Gravel path behind the visitor center
Elevation gain: 281 feet
Distance: 1.9-mile lollipop
Difficulty: Easy
Hiking time: About 1.5 hours
Seasons: Year-round
Schedule: Open daily, 8 a.m. to dusk
Fees and permits: Donations encouraged
Trail contact: Locust Grove Estate, 2683 South Rd., Poughkeepsie, NY 12601; (845) 454-4500; lgny.org

Dog-friendly: Dogs permitted on leash (Please clean up and carry out any waste.)
Trail surface: Gravel, crushed stone, dirt
Land status: Not-for-profit museum and nature preserve
Nearest town: Poughkeepsie, New York
Other trail users: Hikers only; vehicles and bicycles not permitted
Maps: NatGeo TOPO! Map (USGS): Poughkeepsie, NY; trail map available online at lgny.org/wp-content/uploads/2011/10/trailmap.pdf

FINDING THE TRAILHEAD
From the New York State Thruway (I-87), take exit 18 for New Paltz. After the toll plaza, turn right onto NY 299 East. Continue 5 miles to US 9W South. Turn right and continue 2.5 miles. At the ramp for the Mid-Hudson Bridge, turn right and cross the bridge. Immediately turn right onto US 9 south. Drive 2 miles and turn right at the second traffic light into the Locust Grove parking lot. The address is 2683 South Rd., Poughkeepsie, NY. **Metro-North:** Poughkeepsie Station; take a taxi 2 miles to the estate.
Trailhead GPS: N41 40.297' / W73 55.806'

WHAT TO SEE
If you had to memorize Morse code as a Boy or Girl Scout or as part of your military training, you will enjoy this visit to the estate of the code's creator. Not only did Samuel Morse develop the code that became the universal standard for electromagnetic messaging in the first half of the nineteenth century, but he also invented the single-wire telegraph, the first system to transmit a message electronically. He worked closely with Leonard Gale, a professor at New York University, and a young scientist named Alfred Vail to develop relays—connecting circuits that provided the energy to continue

Nicely groomed carriage roads typify the hike at Locust Grove.

a transmission over many miles. Morse's tireless efforts to gain federal funding to build a national telegraph system eventually bore fruit, and the Magnetic Telegraph Company erected some 12,000 miles of telegraph lines across the United States by 1850.

In 1851 Morse and his family moved into the estate at Locust Grove, an Italianate mansion designed by architect A. J. Davis. Here in Poughkeepsie, Morse put his creativity to work in sculpting the gardens and grounds of his home, creating natural settings in which he, his family, and visitors could relax and enjoy the striking view from this bluff over the Hudson River. He used the inspiration of nineteenth-century garden styles of the time, imbuing the grounds with a sense of the romantic as well as a practical kitchen garden.

In 1895 William and Martha Young purchased Locust Grove from Morse's heirs and began to expand the property by purchasing adjoining land. They developed the carriage roads that have become the trails you will follow, rejuvenated the gardens, and created additional beds of their own. The Perennial Garden you see near the villa preserves Martha Young's work and many of her original plantings; the Heritage Kitchen Garden provides a sense of Young's devotion to fresh produce raised on the premises.

In 1975 Annette Innis Young, the last of the Youngs to live at the estate, created a nonprofit organization to continue to run the estate as a museum and historical site. The organization's administrators acquired more land from the adjacent Southwood and Edgehill estates to bring the total property up to 200 acres.

Your hike takes you through all these areas, beginning in the formal gardens and wandering from the carriage road to a high bluff where you can view the river and the

The inventor of Morse code and the telegraph lived in this mansion.

Relax at the pond before continuing to the end of the trail.

passage of trains on the Metro–North rail line. The loop trail then circles back through delightfully cool woods before returning to the parking area.

MILES AND DIRECTIONS

0.0 Start from the parking area and go through the visitor center (or around it if it is closed) to the gravel path. When you reach the garden, turn right on the gravel path. The mansion comes into view on the left. Continue on the path toward the mansion.

0.2 Turn left to go to the mansion. Complete the loop that goes through the entryway to get a good look at the mansion from the outside.

0.3 Turn left at the pet cemetery to start the hiking trail. Another section of the cemetery comes up on your right as you go down the hill.

0.4 Push open the gate and go through. After the gate, take the trail that bears right. This is the Lane Loop.

0.5 An old stone farm wall on the left begins at the posted building. Cross a little stream. In a moment the Lakeside Trail goes left and Edgehill Road goes right. Continue straight.

0.8 The trail forms a T at Sunfish Cove. You may spot a train going through just below. When you're ready, turn left to continue the loop. Soon there's a clearing where you have an unobstructed view of the Hudson River (and the railroad tracks).

0.9 The Sawmill Trail goes right. Continue left on the Lane Loop. Shortly the Sawmill Trail loops back and meets the trail again. Continue straight.

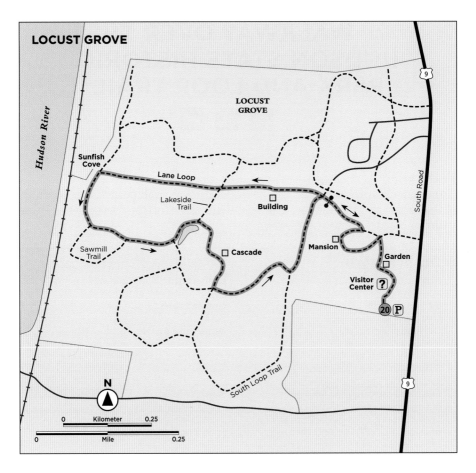

LOCUST GROVE

LOCUST GROVE

Hudson River

Sunfish Cove

Lane Loop

Lakeside Trail

□ Building

Sawmill Trail

□ Cascade

Mansion

Garden

South Road

9

Visitor Center ?

20 P

South Loop Trail

9

N

| 0 | Kilometer | 0.25 |

| 0 | Mile | 0.25 |

1.0 The Lakeside Trail goes left here at the small lake. Turn left on the sunny, mowed grass path. Watch right for a view of the mansion at the top of its hill.

1.1 The Cascade Trail goes right; the Lakeside Trail continues straight. Go right. In a moment you'll come to a trickle of water passing through a stone wall. This is not the promised cascade. Keep going around the bend to the real cascade, with a bridge you can stand on to view it.

1.2 Turn left to rejoin the Lane Loop.

1.4 The South Loop trail goes right. Continue straight (bear left) toward the house.

1.5 At the gate, turn right to return to your vehicle.

1.9 Arrive back at the parking area.

21. WALKWAY OVER THE HUDSON STATE HISTORIC PARK AND LOOP TRAIL

WHY GO?

Cross a brilliantly repurposed railroad bridge high above the Hudson River, and cross back on the Mid-Hudson Bridge for some of the valley's most spectacular views.

THE RUNDOWN

Start: 60 Parker Ave. in Poughkeepsie
Elevation gain: 363 feet
Distance: 4.2-mile loop
Difficulty: Moderate
Hiking time: About 2.5 hours
Seasons: Best Apr–Nov
Schedule: Open daily, sunrise to sunset
Fees and permits: No fees or permits required
Trail contact: New York State Office of Parks, Recreation, and Historic Preservation; (845) 834-2867; nysparks.state.ny.us/parks/178/details.aspx
Dog-friendly: Dogs permitted on leash
Trail surface: Concrete and man-made materials, including sidewalks and roads

Land status: New York state park and municipal public roads
Nearest town: Poughkeepsie, New York
Other trail users: Joggers, families with strollers, dog walkers, wheelchairs, cyclists, inline skaters; vehicular traffic on Mid-Hudson Bridge
Maps: NatGeo TOPO! Map (USGS): Poughkeepsie, NY; interactive map available online at walkway.org
Special considerations: The concrete walkway can be very hot in summer, with little or no shade. If you bring your dog, bring a water bowl and water, and be ready to carry a small dog if the pavement becomes too hot. No skateboards are permitted.

FINDING THE TRAILHEAD

The parking area is at 60 Parker Ave. in Poughkeepsie. *Traveling south on US 9 from Hyde Park*, turn left at the junction with NY 9G and follow 9G until it becomes Parker Avenue. Parking is on the left in about 0.2 mile.

Traveling north on US 9, turn right on NY 55 in Poughkeepsie and take US 44/NY 55 North at Washington Street. Continue north on Washington to Parker Avenue and turn right. The parking lot is on the left in about 0.02 mile.

Trailhead GPS: N41 42.749' / W73 55.585'

WHAT TO SEE

If you only hike one trail in the Hudson River Valley, the Walkway Over the Hudson may be the one for you. Whether you choose to hike the entire loop or simply walk out onto the former Poughkeepsie-Highland Railroad Bridge to take in the amazing river views, you will have no finer opportunity to appreciate the Hudson River and its beautiful valley than from this vantage point.

An inspired repurposing of an industrial bridge, the Walkway Over the Hudson puts back into use a nineteenth-century railroad bridge that served as a major rail corridor for many decades. The Poughkeepsie-Highland Railroad Bridge stood as the longest bridge in the world when it opened on January 1, 1889—a $3.6 million project that was the first to cross the Hudson River between New York City and Albany. Freight trains carrying iron and lumber, passenger trains from as far north as Boston and heading as far south as Washington, and so-called "rapid transit" trolley cars filled with tourists and students all passed over this bridge. Over the years the bridge saw livestock, circus trains, and even football fans on their way to and from West Point cross the Hudson on its expanse. At the bridge's peak usage, more than 3,500 rail cars crossed it every day.

When fire severely damaged the bridge in 1974, the remains of the old structure stood dormant until a group of enthusiastic citizens came together with state and federal governments to repair the bridge and transform it into a new state park. The $38.8 million project was actually less expensive than demolishing the damaged bridge—an effort that would have required $50 million to complete. Today the park contains the world's longest pedestrian bridge at 1.28 miles, at a height of 212 feet above the Hudson River.

An ingeniously repurposed railroad bridge is the centerpiece of the Walkway Over the Hudson.

THE FRANKLIN D. ROOSEVELT MID-HUDSON BRIDGE

With so much focus on the repurposed Poughkeepsie-Highland Railroad Bridge, you may not have taken a good, close look at the Mid-Hudson Bridge recently. It might come as a surprise, then, that the Mid-Hudson—designed in the 1920s by Ralph Modjeski, who also worked on the Poughkeepsie-Highland Railroad Bridge—was hailed as the most beautiful suspension bridge in the region when it opened in 1930. Naming the bridge for former governor Franklin D. Roosevelt did not take place until 1994, when the New York State Legislature chose to remember the former governor with this honor.

Five years later, in 1999, the public welcomed the newly constructed Mid-Hudson Bridge Scenic Walkway, allowing pedestrians to cross the bridge safely for the first time—the only place they could do so between Newburgh and Hudson. This paved the way (literally) for the loop trail you can walk today, crossing two monumental bridges and enjoying the spectacular views from each.

The wide, smooth, modern walkway opened on October 3, 2009, and now stands as the longest elevated pedestrian bridge in the world. Visitors can stroll 212 feet above the river's surface and admire a spectacular view of the river to the north and south. A sunny summer Sunday can draw thousands of people to the park, making downtown Poughkeepsie a new meeting place for neighbors and friends throughout the Hudson River Valley.

Recognizing the value of a longer walk for energetic hikers, the state park has designated a loop trail that crosses both this bridge and the Mid-Hudson Bridge about 0.5 mile south. A highly trafficked segment of US 44 and NY 55, the Mid-Hudson

The walkway elevates visitors above the Hudson River shoreline.

Bridge has a pedestrian walkway and an attraction of its own: *Bridge Music*, the remarkable accomplishment of composer Joseph Bertolozzi. The sounds of traffic crossing the bridge inspired Bertolozzi to write a series of pieces that can be described as percussive funk, created using only the sounds he could generate by making the bridge itself his drum kit. You can listen to a wide selection of these jazzy pieces when you reach the Mid-Hudson Bridge arches, where you will find speakers and buttons to push to hear Bertolozzi's compositions.

MILES AND DIRECTIONS

0.0 Start from the parking area and head west on the walkway. Pass through shady woods and over a Poughkeepsie neighborhood before the bridge begins to cross the river. You'll find food concessions here. Once you're on the bridge, the walk across the bridge continues for 1.28 miles.

1.5 The bridge ends here. The walkway continues to your left (southwest) on a paved path. There's parking on this side of the bridge as well. Turn left at the end of the parking area, and continue to walk down the access road. US 44 and NY 55 are on your right.

2.1 At the end of the access road, you'll find Johnson-Iorio Memorial Park. There's a parking area here with interpretive signage about the Mid-Hudson Bridge. Turn left onto the bridge's pedestrian walkway. You're separated from the car traffic by guardrails and steel grating.

2.2 Here's the first *Bridge Music* listening post, on the first arch. You'll also see signs here about peregrine falcons nesting on this arch; if you're here between February and June, keep an eye out for peregrines flying around this post.

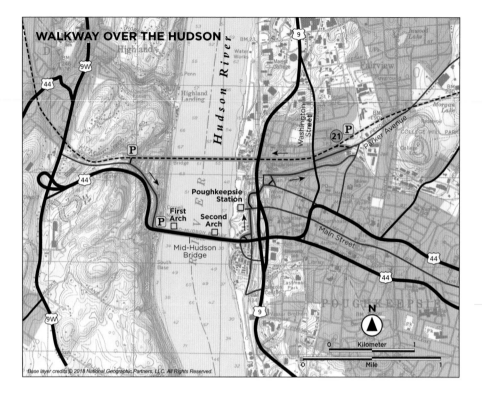

2.5 The second arch has another listening post. You're welcome to linger on the bridge, admire the view, and listen to the music for as long as you like.

2.8 At the end of the bridge, turn left on the walkway trail. The route will be obvious; the sidewalk is fenced here and descends to street level. When you reach Rinaldi Boulevard, turn left.

2.9 Turn right on Main Street. At this corner there's a plaza with several restaurants adjacent to Poughkeepsie Station's pedestrian walkway. You may want to stop here for lunch, ice cream, or a smoothie. When you're ready, continue to the covered pedestrian walkway and turn left onto the walkway. Continue into the station and turn right. Pass the ticket counter and snack bar, and come out on the east side of the station. Continue north on the sidewalk to Davies Place.

3.0 When you reach Dongen Park, turn right onto Dongen Place. Continue through the park to Mill Street.

3.3 Turn left on Mill Street and continue to Verazzano Boulevard. Turn right on Verazzano.

3.4 Turn left on Washington Street.

3.8 Turn right on Parker Avenue. Continue on Parker to the parking area.

4.2 Arrive back at the parking area.

22. PEACH HILL PARK

WHY GO?
Climb through meadows, orchards, and successional woods to summit the highest hill in Poughkeepsie.

THE RUNDOWN

Start: Parking area at 32 Edgewood Dr. in Poughkeepsie
Elevation gain: 269 feet
Distance: 2.1-mile loop
Difficulty: Moderate
Hiking time: About 1.5 hours
Seasons: Year-round; best in spring when the apple blossoms are in bloom and in fall when the leaves are changing
Schedule: Open daily, 7 a.m. to dusk
Fees and permits: No fees or permits required
Trail contact: Town of Poughkeepsie Recreation Department, 1 Overocker Rd., Poughkeepsie, NY 12603; (845) 485-3628; peach-hill-park.org
Dog-friendly: Dogs permitted on leash
Trail surface: Mowed grass
Land status: Town of Poughkeepsie

Nearest town: Poughkeepsie, New York
Other trail users: Trail runners
Maps: NatGeo TOPO! Map (USGS): Poughkeepsie, NY; trail map available online at peach-hill-park.org/trail-map
Special considerations: Stay in the middle of the mowed grass path to avoid poison ivy and reduce contact with ticks. The park brochure adds this warning: "The park was formerly an apple orchard where agricultural pesticides were used. Such pesticides may present a health risk if ingested. Please remain on marked trails and do not come in direct contact with the soil." I clarified this with the park: Don't eat the soil. So if you pick up an apple from the ground, wash off any soil before eating it.

FINDING THE TRAILHEAD
In Poughkeepsie, take Smith Street to the Salt Point Turnpike. Turn right on the turnpike and watch for NY 115 North. Turn left onto NY 115 and continue 1.5 miles to Edgewood Drive. Turn right onto Edgewood and continue to the parking area.
Trailhead GPS: N41 43.823' / W73 52.836'

WHAT TO SEE
You may not guess that a 485-foot "summit" would be quite as much of a workout as this trail turns out to be, but it will get your heart pumping as you trek to the highest point in Poughkeepsie. The trail provides a steady upward climb for nearly a mile, culminating in a pretty darned good view just after you reach the top. No, the view isn't

The mowed path leads to the top of Peach Hill.

at the summit—there's a nice little sign there letting you know that you made it to the high point, but the viewpoints actually come along a little while later, as you start down.

We took the History Trail to the top, but as there were no interpretive signs explaining what the history might be, let me fill you in. In the 1930s the area now included in Peach Hill Park consisted of fields, meadows, woods, and a small orchard. A farmer named Charles Beck bought up the land in 1948 and turned it into apple, peach, and pear orchards, giving the hill its evocative name. Over the next two decades, the peach and pear trees eventually were replaced by apple varieties. In 1967 William Paladino Jr. purchased the property and added even more apple trees, bringing the total to at least 10,000. The hill operated as a working orchard until 1999.

In 2000, with open space dwindling in the Hudson Valley and residential and commercial development encroaching on the Peach Hill orchards, a group of concerned citizens stepped up to protect the property in perpetuity. Scenic Hudson, Dutchess County, New York State, and the Town of Poughkeepsie joined with this community group to acquire the property and turn it into a park, completing the necessary transactions in 2004 and opening the orchards, adjoining woodlands, and meadows to the public to enjoy—while creating no burden for local taxpayers. The Friends of Peach Hill remains the fundraising organization for this park, providing for its maintenance. You can thank them for the nicely mowed and well-defined trail you will follow on your hike, as well as for the

You've reached the summit. Take a moment to determine your return route.

SUMMIT OF
PEACH HILL

ELEVATION 485 FEET

HIGHEST POINT IN
TOWN OF POUGHKEEPSIE

The Hudson Valley view can be found at viewpoints below the summit.

interpretive materials at the overlooks and the benches and picnic tables you will be oh so grateful to find at the top of the hill.

A word about the orchards: The absolute best time to hike Peach Hill is when the apple trees are in bloom, usually from late April to early May. If you hike in late summer, however, you will certainly come upon trees laden with fresh fruit. The park's instruction on this is simple: "Leave nothing but footprints; take nothing but memories . . . and apples." Go ahead and gather as many as you like. Two areas of the orchard are pruned and maintained by the Friends to produce apples without pesticides (you'll pass one of these on the orange trail). You'll find Winesap, Red Delicious, White Delicious, and McIntosh apples in this orchard.

MILES AND DIRECTIONS

0.0   Start at the south side of the parking lot on a wide gravel path. You'll take the red (History) trail up and the orange (Geology) trail down. On the red trail, take an immediate right onto the mowed grass path. Start going up.

0.1   The green trail goes left. Continue straight on the red trail.

0.3   High-tension wires go through this utility right-of-way.

0.7   An unmarked mowed grass path goes left. Continue straight on the red trail.

0.8   The white trail goes left here. Continue straight.

1.1   There's a bench at this left turn. From here it's a rise of about 130 feet, so feel free to take a rest.

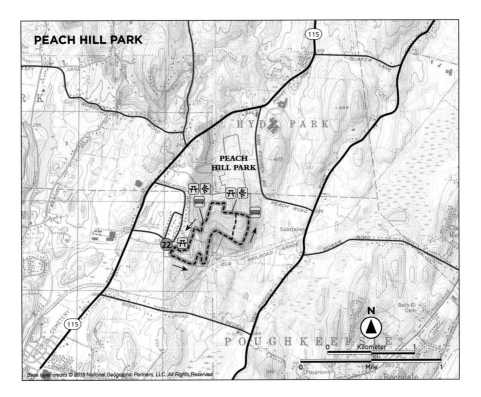

1.2 Trails meet in this clearing. Red continues to the right (up). Soon you'll come to a picnic table at a nice viewpoint looking east.

1.3 Here is the summit, at 485 feet. There is no view here, so take the orange trail to the next clearing. The trails here are a little tricky. With your back to the summit sign (or sitting on the bench), there appears to be three trails in front of you. Red goes to your left, and white, green, and orange are together in one trail. Take this combined trail down.

1.5 At the Y junction, go right to follow the orange trail. Immediately arrive at the Catskill Overlook. When you're ready, head left to continue on the orange trail.

1.6 Reach the Mid-Hudson Overlook. Look for two orange markers with black arrows to continue on the orange trail.

1.7 The orange trail turns right.

1.8 At this junction, the orange, green, and blue trails all join and continue straight.

1.9 The orange trail turns right at this junction. One of the "model orchards" is on the left.

2.0 Come to a picnic area. Follow the crushed stone path through here to the parking area.

2.1 Arrive back at the parking area.

23. HYDE PARK TRAIL: ROOSEVELT AND VANDERBILT NATIONAL HISTORIC SITES

WHY GO?

Our nation's only four-term president left us this uncommonly lovely woodland and the carriage roads that bring us to its verdant heart. His wealthy neighbors preserved an equally fine natural oasis.

THE RUNDOWN

Start: Roosevelt Farm Lane parking area

Elevation gain: 298 feet

Distance: 9.3 miles one-way, including two loops with a long connector (shuttle recommended) (2.7-mile lollipop for Farm Lane only)

Difficulty: Moderate

Hiking time: About 4 hours

Seasons: Year-round except in deep snow

Schedule: Open daily, sunrise to sunset

Fees and permits: No charge to walk the trail; fee to visit the presidential library, FDR's home, and the Vanderbilt mansion.

Trail contact: Home of Franklin Delano Roosevelt National Historic Site, 4079 Albany Post Rd., Hyde Park, NY 12538; (845) 229-9115; nps .gov/hofr

Vanderbilt Mansion National Historic Site, 4097 Albany Post Rd.,

Hyde Park, NY 12538; (845) 229-9115; nps.gov/vama

Dog-friendly: Dogs permitted on leash

Trail surface: Crushed stone, dirt and mowed-grass path, some paved road

Land status: National historic sites, a short stretch of public road

Nearest town: Hyde Park, New York

Other trail users: Trail runners; cross-country skiers in season

Maps: NatGeo TOPO! Map (USGS): Hyde Park, NY; National Park Service and Hyde Park Trail maps available at the Henry A. Wallace Visitor Center at Franklin D. Roosevelt Presidential Library and Museum or online at nps .gov/elro/planyourvisit/things2do .htm and hydeparkny.us/Recreation/ Trails/

Special considerations: Take precautions against ticks and poison ivy.

FINDING THE TRAILHEAD

From Manhattan, take the Henry Hudson Parkway north to the Taconic Parkway; continue to I-84 West. Take I-84 to US 9 North. The FDR presidential library is on the left side of US 9, 4 miles north of Poughkeepsie. Roosevelt Farm Lane is on the right side of NY 9, directly across from the home and library.

From Albany, take the New York State Thruway (1-87) south to exit 18 at New Paltz. Take the exit and follow NY 299 East to US 9W South. Cross the Mid-Hudson Bridge

and continue to US 9 North. The home and library are on the left side of US 9; Roosevelt Farm Lane is on the right side of NY 9, directly across from the library.

To make this a shuttle hike, leave your second car at Vanderbilt Mansion, 119 Vanderbilt Park Rd., about 2.7 miles north of Roosevelt Farm Lane on US 9. GPS: N41 48.121' / W73 56.465'

Trailhead GPS: N41 46.194' / W73 55.784'

WHAT TO SEE

For national park units per square mile, Hyde Park rivals Washington, DC, in its work to preserve important slices of American history. Here the lives of several of the wealthiest families in the nation played out during the late 1800s and the first half of the twentieth century, as they applied some of the Vanderbilts' railroad money and the Roosevelts' financial legacy to cultivate the natural areas we see today.

You can drive from one historic site to the next, of course, but the town of Hyde Park has established a well-marked and nicely maintained trail system that allows you to turn your visit into an all-day hiking experience. I recommend parking a car at the Roosevelt Farm and Forest parking area and another one at the Vanderbilt Mansion. Each of these sites provides a loop trail of its own, with the lengthier connecting trail winding through the Home of Franklin Delano Roosevelt National Historic Site and on into a Hyde Park residential area. It arrives at the southern end of the Vanderbilt Mansion National Historic Site, where you will discover some particularly pleasant waterfalls that most guests never see.

Now for some historical context before you begin your exploration. If you weren't around during the Great Depression or World War II, Franklin Delano Roosevelt's name may be no more to you than one in a list of forty-odd presidents of the United States. For history enthusiasts and those who lived during his four-term presidency, however, the list of Roosevelt's accomplishments extends well beyond the pages of any textbook—and one of the least known of these is his devotion to conservation, well before the environment became a fashionable cause.

We are fortunate to be able to enjoy the literal fruits of Roosevelt's land preservation efforts here at the last remaining acres of his own farm and forest, saved from development in 2004 by the Scenic Hudson Land Trust and now preserved by the National Park Service. Just across the street, the Home of Franklin D. Roosevelt National Historic Site tells the fascinating story of the president's battle with polio, his life outside the White House, and his relationship with his wife, venerable First Lady Eleanor Roosevelt. The FDR Presidential Library and Museum fill in all the blanks about the successes that brought this president four terms in the White House: the establishment of Social Security, the New Deal that hastened the end of the Depression, creation of the Civilian Conservation Corps, and his leadership during World War II, to name just a few.

Roosevelt developed an interest in birds and trees as a youth, riding on horseback and wandering throughout the family estate. His interest was further inspired by the conservation work of his uncle, Theodore Roosevelt, who (among other things) created the USDA Forest Service. When FDR was elected to the New York State Senate in 1911,

Ponds and streams create an idyllic environment on the Vanderbilt estate.

he chaired the senate's Forest, Fish and Game Commission, and he began to apply to his own lands the principles of scientific forestry—the management of a sustainable timber crop with a careful balance between environmental protection and harvesting. At his direction, more than half a million trees were planted on his property here in Hyde Park, creating the strikingly beautiful woodland that surrounds this trail. This mixed forest features many species that are native to the Hudson River Valley: beech, poplar, tulip tree, maple, and oak, as well as eastern hemlock and other conifers. The forest floor's carpet of ferns and many naturally occurring broadleaf plants is unusually lovely—the result of smart, health-enriching forestry practices.

The opulence you'll find on the Vanderbilt estate came from the fortune amassed by the Vanderbilt family, who owned the New York Central Railroad. Frederick Vanderbilt was one of the directors of the railroad for sixty-one years and its president for a brief time. The mansion and estate had fallen into disrepair when the Vanderbilts purchased it, but Frederick saw the potential in restoring this natural setting and its expansive grounds. Today you get to see the Hudson Valley the way the richest of the rich saw it more than one hundred years ago.

MILES AND DIRECTIONS

0.0 Start at the parking lot. The Farm Lane carriage trail leads east. You'll see Hyde Park Trail markers: a white disk with a green tulip tree leaf.

0.3 The Red Trail goes left here (it's marked with a wooden sign). Continue straight. In about 30 steps, a path goes right. You will see many of these unmarked paths as you walk down the carriage road.

0.6 The Yellow Trail goes off to the left here. Continue on the Farm Lane (bear right at the fork). A stream flows to your left.

0.9 Cross a bridge over a gentle stream (the Maritje Kill). Just after the bridge, a side trail goes left. Continue straight.

1.4 The Yellow Trail begins to your left. Turn left onto the Yellow trail. Follow the yellow blazes on trees, every 20 yards or so.

1.5 The Blue Trail goes right. Continue straight on the Yellow Trail. Note the eastern hemlocks in this section of the woods, lining both sides of the trail.

1.8 At the trail intersection, go left on the Yellow Trail then left again at the second intersection (just after you cross the stream).

1.9 The Red Trail begins on your right. Turn right and follow the Red Trail. You'll see red blazes on the trees.

2.2 At the trail junction, take the left fork and continue to follow the Red Trail.

2.3 At the junction with three red blazes, turn left.

2.4 You've returned to the Farm Lane carriage road. Turn right on the carriage road and return to the parking lot.

2.7 You've reached your vehicle. If you've had enough, you can stop here. If you're ready to continue, proceed across Albany Post Road to the Home of FDR National Historic Site.

2.9 This is the parking area for the FDR Presidential Library and visitor center. Take the paved path that begins at the south side of the parking area, and follow signs for the Hyde Park Trail.

3.0 Turn right on the gravel path after the fenced garden. At the Y junction, go left (down) on the paved path, again following the Hyde Park Trail tulip tree markers.

3.1 A gravel path goes left. The paved road goes right to a park residence. Go left.

3.2 Bear right on the Hyde Park Trail (white-and-green markers with a tulip tree leaf logo). You've been walking on a country road with a meadow and orchard on your left and woods on the right. Look up and left over the meadow to see FDR's mansion (which may be barely visible in spring and summer).

3.3 Come to a stream with a dam. In spring there is enough water flow to create a cascade.

3.4 At the Y junction, follow the Hyde Park Trail right; the Meadow Trail (yellow markers) goes left. Soon a pond appears to the left. Wild yellow lily grows here, as well as wild geranium.

The mostly level trail winds through woods, follows streambeds, and crosses roads.

3.8 The Forest Trail loop (green markers) goes right, and the Hyde Park Trail goes left. Go left.

4.2 You are leaving the national park. Go left at the signpost to stay on the Hyde Park Trail toward the Vanderbilt estate. At the Y junction, bear right (follow the Hyde Park Trail signs). The Hudson River is visible to the left through the trees. This is rolling, wooded terrain, but the hills are gentle.

4.7 Emerge from the woods on a paved, open turnaround area at the end of a road. This is River Road, a residential area. Look down at the pavement for the white Hyde Park Trail emblem, with arrows for the Vanderbilt and FDR sites. Follow the arrow to the Vanderbilt estate (straight ahead).

5.3 Turn left here into Riverfront Park, and continue through the park by turning right. There's a playground, picnic tables, and railroad trains at close range. On the trail, steps lead down into the playground. Walk through the playground, past the pavilion, and through the parking area.

5.4 Arrive at the Historic Hyde Park train station. From here, head back to the road and continue uphill (follow the white emblem on the road surface).

5.6 You've reached Dock Street. The Dock Street bridge is closed to both vehicles and pedestrians, but from the stone wall at the roadside, you can see the waterfall created by a dam here. Look upstream for a second waterfall (stand in front of the "Dead End" sign for the best view). When ready, return to River Road and continue left to the entrance to the Vanderbilt estate.

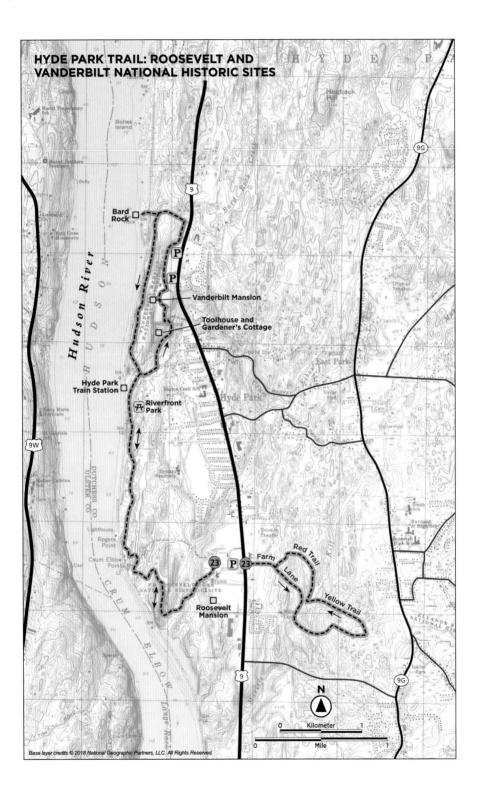

HYDE PARK TRAIL: ROOSEVELT AND VANDERBILT NATIONAL HISTORIC SITES

Bard Rock

P

P

Vanderbilt Mansion

Toolhouse and Gardener's Cottage

Hyde Park Train Station

Riverfront Park

Hudson River

9

9G

9W

23 P 23 Farm Lane

Red Trail

Yellow Trail

Roosevelt Mansion

9

9G

N

Kilometer

0   1

Mile

0   1

Base layer credits © 2018 National Geographic Partners, LLC. All Rights Reserved.

5.8 At Coach House Drive, turn left to enter Vanderbilt National Historic Site. Pass the coach house and cross the stone bridge. Stop to view the long series of chute waterfalls. At the end of the bridge, turn right on the one-way paved road.

6.1 The Toolhouse and Gardener's Cottage are visible on your left. Continue straight. Across the road, a stone bridge and a dam create a beautiful photo opportunity. When you reach the bridge, turn left, cross the road, and take the gravel path. When you reach the paved loop, turn left to walk past the mansion.

6.3 Arrive at the mansion.

6.5 South end of the parking area. You can return to your car here and end your hike, or continue to the Vanderbilt loop trail. If you're continuing, cross the parking areas to the north end, where the loop begins.

6.8 The road at the north end of the parking area goes straight (north) and to the right (east). Continue straight toward Bard Rock.

7.0 Leave the road and take the path to your left. Descend on the path and meet up with the road again. (**Option:** You can skip this shorter path and continue to walk on the road.) Follow the road down to the west, toward the river. The open field to your left is home to goldfinches, meadowlarks, tree swallows, and many other birds.

7.2 A path goes left here. This is the Hyde Park Trail; you'll come back to this shortly. For now, continue straight to enjoy the view from Bard Rock. Cross the one-lane bridge.

7.3 Reach Bard Rock. The view of the river here is unsurpassed. (There's parking here, if you want to return with your vehicle at another time.) When you're ready, turn around and go back across the one-lane bridge to the Hyde Park Trail.

7.4 Turn right on the Hyde Park Trail and begin walking through the woods.

8.1 Vanderbilt Mansion comes into view on the left.

8.2 The trail to the left is a shortcut to the gardens and parking area. Continue straight.

8.6 Cross the chain barrier and continue to the road. At the road, turn left (there's an exit gate to your right).

8.7 Take the trail to your left, back into the woods. Begin a short but pronounced ascent. The trail levels off shortly.

8.9 You've arrived at the Vanderbilt formal gardens. Take some time here to stroll through and enjoy the variety of shrubs and flowers.

9.1 Reach the south entrance to Vanderbilt Mansion. Bear right on the gravel path around the building. Cross the pavement and continue north on the gravel path toward the parking area.

9.2 Continue north on the sidewalk. At the visitor center, turn right and proceed to the parking lot.

9.3 Arrive at the beginning of the spacious parking area. Continue across it to your shuttle vehicle.

24. TOP COTTAGE AND ELEANOR ROOSEVELT ESTATE

WHY GO?

Hike through the forest planted on orders from President Franklin Delano Roosevelt, and follow the swath cut by the twentieth century's strongest and most influential First Lady.

THE RUNDOWN

Start: To the right after you cross the bridge at Eleanor Roosevelt National Historic Site in Hyde Park, on your way to the visitor center and Val-Kill
Elevation gain: 238 feet
Distance: 3.1 miles out and back
Hiking time: About 1.5 hours
Seasons: Spring through fall
Schedule: Trail open daily, sunrise to sunset
Difficulty: Moderate
Fees and permits: No charge to hike the trail; fee to tour Val-Kill
Trail contacts: The Roosevelt-Vanderbilt National Historic Sites,
4097 Albany Post Rd., Hyde Park, NY 12538; (845) 229-9115, ext. 2010; nps.gov/elro
Dog-friendly: Dogs on leash on trails only; no pets in the historic buildings
Trail surface: Dirt and woodland detritus
Land status: National Park Service
Nearest town: Hyde Park, New York
Other trail users: Hikers only
Maps: NatGeo TOPO! Map (USGS): Hyde Park, NY; trail maps available from the National Park Service at nps.gov/elro/planyourvisit/things2do.htm

FINDING THE TRAILHEAD

From the New York State Thruway (I-87), take exit 18 for New Paltz. Take NY 299 East to US 9W South, and follow the signs to the Mid-Hudson Bridge (FDR Bridge). Cross the bridge and follow the signs to US 9 North. Drive 3 miles on US 9 North until you see the Culinary Institute of America. At the first traffic light after the CIA, turn right onto St. Andrews Road. When St. Andrews ends, turn left onto NY 9G North. Drive 0.5 mile to the entrance to Val-Kill. The address is 54 Valkill Park Rd., Hyde Park, New York. Park in the lot before the bridge to the visitor center and Val-Kill cottage.
Trailhead GPS: N41 45.702' / W73 54.015'

WHAT TO SEE

It's not every day that you can walk in the footsteps of a First Lady of the United States, so we urge you to seize the opportunity here at Val-Kill. This is the cottage at which Eleanor Roosevelt, wife of President Franklin Delano Roosevelt, pursued her many

Walk in the footsteps of Eleanor Roosevelt along this trail on her estate.

Once you get to Top Cottage up the challenging trail, you can relax on the porch.

Top Cottage was Franklin Roosevelt's home away from home.

humanitarian causes and entertained world leaders who came to pay their respects at the grave of her husband. Mrs. Roosevelt walked often in the woods near her cottage, making this a place to contemplate the extraordinary achievements of the woman whom President Harry S. Truman called "First Lady of the World."

The loop trail called Eleanor's Walk offers a vigorous stroll through healthy woodland, with a short, steep change in elevation as you approach a pond. Once you've completed the short loop, we recommend continuing on the Top Cottage Trail, a challenging uphill hike to the house FDR had constructed so he could "escape the mob" of favor-seekers who crowded his calendar throughout his presidency. FDR himself drove his car up this winding road to Top Cottage—back when this road was passable by car. A section of FDR's original road was replaced by a housing development, so today's route to Top Cottage is a footpath that detours past that section—a rocky, heart-pumping climb to the top of the Roosevelt estate.

The two small houses at this historic site tell us a great deal about the relationship between Franklin and Eleanor Roosevelt before and during FDR's presidency. Val-Kill, constructed on land Franklin gave his wife as a gift, became the home Eleanor shared on weekends with her friends and political coworkers Nancy Cook and Marion Dicker-man beginning in 1925. Here Eleanor could get some separation from her domineering mother-in-law and pursue her own interests, including Val-Kill Industries, a manufac-turing business in which farm workers learned marketable skills by making furniture, woven pieces, and pewter household items. When Eleanor became First Lady in 1933, she maintained Val-Kill and its manufacturing buildings as a place to carry on her work whenever she visited Hyde Park—and here she entertained heads of state including British Prime Minister Winston Churchill, the Netherlands' Queen Wilhelmina, First Secretary of the Communist Party of the Soviet Union Nikita Khrushchev, Ethiopian Emperor Haile Selassie, Yugoslavian Chairman Josip Broz Tito, and Jawaharlal Nehru, prime minister of India.

At Top Cottage, FDR and his longtime friend and companion Margaret "Daisy" Suckley designed a place for the president to take refuge from the constant barrage of politicians, petitioners, and other visitors who took his open-door policy to an unbearable extreme. Here he worked, read, spent some precious leisure time, and occasionally entertained heads of state including Crown Prince Olav V and Princess Martha of Norway, Winston Churchill, Madame Chiang Kai-shek of China, Crown Princess Louise of Sweden, and Mackenzie King, prime minister of Canada. He also spent time on his back porch admiring the more than half a million trees planted on the hillsides and in the valley below, and watching birds among the leaves and branches at the perfect angle for spotting them.

MILES AND DIRECTIONS

0.0 Start at the parking lot entrance, turn right, and follow the signs for Hyde Park Trail. Cross the bridge over the brook. This is the Fall Kill, for which Val-Kill is named ("kill" is Dutch for "creek").

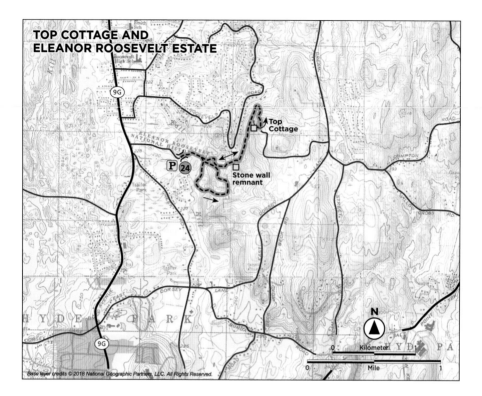

0.1 Turn right from the road onto the Hyde Park Trail. Cross the parking area to the trailhead for Eleanor's Walk/Top Cottage Trail. Follow Eleanor's Walk (red blazes), bearing right.

0.6 After a steady incline, there's a pond to your right.

1.1 You've completed the Eleanor's Walk loop. Turn right for the Top Cottage Trail (green-and-white Hyde Park Trail markers).

1.4 Cross over the first of several stone wall remnants and start uphill.

2.0 Reach the top of the hill, where the trail ends at a mowed area. Top Cottage is straight ahead. If you collect National Park Passport stamps, there's one here for the Hudson River Valley National Heritage Area. If you're lucky enough to arrive during a ranger-guided public tour, you may join in, if there is room. When you've had a chance to visit with the ranger and tour the cottage, head back down the way you came.

2.9 You are back at the trailhead. Continue over the bridge to the parking area.

3.1 Arrive back at the parking area.

25. **FALLING WATERS PRESERVE**

WHY GO?
An open meadow, burbling waterfalls, and wide water views distinguish this delightful protected area on the banks of the Hudson.

THE RUNDOWN

Start: Falling Waters Preserve parking area at 996 Dominican Lane, Glasco

Elevation gain: 172 feet
Distance: 1.6-mile loop
Difficulty: Easy
Hiking time: About 1 hour
Seasons: Year-round
Schedule: Open daily, dawn to dusk
Fees and permits: No fees or permits required; available for special events and group outings: scenichudson.org/whatyoucando/visitourparks/specialeventpermits
Trail contact: Scenic Hudson, One Civic Center Plaza, Suite 200, Poughkeepsie, NY 12601; (845)

473-4440; scenichudson.org/parks/fallingwaters; e-mail: info@scenichudson.org
Dog-friendly: Dogs permitted on 6-foot leash (Please clean up and carry out any waste.)
Trail surface: Packed earth, some potentially muddy parts
Land status: Scenic Hudson Land Trust
Nearest town: Glasco, New York
Other trail users: Hikers only
Maps: NatGeo TOPO! Map (USGS): Saugerties, NY; trail map available online at scenichudson.org/sites/default/files/fallingwaters-2016_webmap.jpg

FINDING THE TRAILHEAD
From Saugerties, drive south on US 9W and bear left on NY 32 South. Take the first left onto Glasco Turnpike. Continue through the village of Glasco, and turn left on York Street. Watch for the sign for Falling Waters Preserve on your right.
From the south, drive north on US 9W, and turn right on CR 32. Continue straight as CR 32 becomes Main Street, and turn left on York Street. Watch for the sign for Falling Waters Preserve on your right.
Trailhead GPS: N42 02.933' / W73 56.439'

WHAT TO SEE
When you visit Falling Waters Preserve and discover the charms of this little sanctuary tucked along the banks of the Hudson, take a moment to consider the good works of the Dominican Sisters of Sparkill, who had the foresight to safeguard this land and make the connection with local land trusts to protect it in perpetuity.

The Dominican Sisters, who live adjacent to the preserve, have a stated Land Ethic as part of their official doctrine. Within this, they underscore their personal commitment to

The waters fall at this preserve in any season.

Pause to reflect when you reach the falling waters.

the preservation of places like this one. "We have come to know Earth as sacred in itself, as revelatory of divinity," the Land Ethic says. "We have come to understand that Earth's benefits are for everyone, that land should be conserved, restored, and shared equitably."

In this spirit, the Dominican Sisters of Sparkill, Scenic Hudson, and Esopus Creek Conservancy formed a unique partnership, and in 2015 Scenic Hudson acquired 149

WHAT ARE THESE SEEDPODS?

Even if you hike along the Hudson River in the dead of winter, you'll see these oddly shaped seedpods with several pointy ends (see top photo on page 157) scattered all over the trail and the surrounding ground. These come from an invasive plant called the European water chestnut—in summer, you can see its green foliage blanketing the water's surface. As attractive as this may seem, the water chestnut is a dangerous invader that prevents sunlight from penetrating the water's surface and draws oxygen out of the water. The native plants that should grow here must fight for survival, and many of them have lost the battle. Fish and other animals that depend on oxygen in the water also have had to move elsewhere.

In its native habitat in Europe and Asia, there are insects that feed on the water chestnut and keep it from overwhelming waterways. These insects do not live in North America, however, so there is no natural enemy of this plant to restore the balance in our ecosystem. Unfortunately, it's not the same water chestnut you find in the Asian section of grocery stores, so it is not generally harvested as a human food source.

Be careful to check your shoelaces, pant legs, and anything else that has touched the ground before you leave the area to be sure you don't give these seedpods a free ride to another environment where their damaging habits can spread.

acres to ensure permanent public access. This gives hikers water-level access to the Hudson River, as well as the woods, streams, waterfall, wetlands, and an open hayfield—something of a rarity along the densely populated river.

The hayfield is of particular interest to birders, as it attracts eastern bluebirds, northern harriers, savannah sparrows, and other grassland birds that struggle to find habitat in suburban areas. The periodically mowed hayfield draws minimal human activity, allowing it to support some grassland breeding birds that get forced out of farmlands by more intensive activity.

The footpath takes you along a ridge that borders the meadow until it reaches a private residence (there's a gate to keep you from accidentally trespassing). Here you will make a right turn and take a short side path to the edge of an unnamed river tributary, where you can stop to enjoy the waterfall rushing over a rocky streambed.

You may notice young trees planted along a stream as you drive toward the parking area. In 2011 Falling Waters Preserve was selected to become a planting site for Trees for Tribs, a New York State Department of Environmental Conservation Hudson River Estuary Program to create "riparian buffers" along tributaries of the river. A riparian area forms an interface of trees and plants between land and a river, using the water to nourish a diverse mix of plant life, which in turn helps prevent erosion. Riparian areas provide shade to water creatures, shelter to birds and animals, food for insects—many of which become food for birds—and they even help remove impurities from the water, improving overall water quality. Scenic Hudson and volunteers care for this planted area to be sure it grows into a healthy ecosystem along the tributary.

While we did not include this in the hike detailed below, a blue-blazed trail goes south from here and leads to the remains of the Mulford Ice House, a building that stored as much as 10,000 tons of ice removed from the river during winter. The ice kept here would be shipped to New York City in spring and summer in the days before refrigerators. The icehouse burned down in 1915, giving conservationists the opportunity to reopen this land to its natural evolution. You can still see bricks from the old icehouse along the trail, but now the floodplain has grown into a forest, providing habitat to uncommon plants and wildlife.

MILES AND DIRECTIONS

0.0 Start at the trailhead in the northeast corner of the parking area. A blue-blazed trail here goes off to the right. Take this for about 100 feet to see the waterfall there and a rustic cedar sitting area. When you're ready, return to the parking area and take the red trail. In a moment the white trail goes right; this is your return route. Continue straight on the red trail.

0.4 At a wooden bench, you can view the open meadow. Watch for eastern bluebirds, eastern kingbirds, and other field birds here.

0.5 Reach a second overlook, where you can see more of the meadow.

0.7 The red trail reaches a wooden gate; the property beyond is private. Turn right on the white trail and you'll see that the red trail continues to your

European water chestnuts

The Hudson River is close enough to touch from the trail.

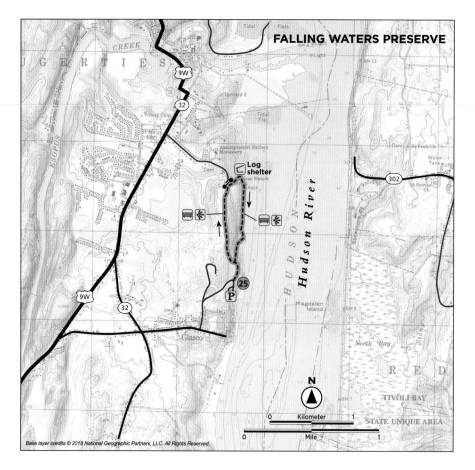

FALLING WATERS PRESERVE

immediate left and leads down to the tributary, where you can see the waterfall.

0.8 Arrive at the waterfall and a log shelter. When you're ready, the trail continues either straight ahead or back the way you came. You will meet the white trail in either direction; continue down to the river's edge.

0.9 A break in the vegetation here gives you a wide view of the Hudson River. From here the trail ascends to a ridgeline.

1.1 A log bench here provides a rest after the uphill stretch. This is another scenic overlook.

1.5 The white trail meets the red trail here. Continue straight on the red trail to reach the parking area.

1.6 Arrive back at the parking area.

26. WINNAKEE NATURE PRESERVE

WHY GO?
Discover a hidden, deliciously green wild space just beyond the strip malls.

THE RUNDOWN

Start: Parking area at the end of Terwilliger Road Extension in Hyde Park
Elevation gain: 77 feet
Distance: 0.8-mile loop
Difficulty: Easy
Hiking time: About 1 hour
Seasons: Year-round
Schedule: Open daily, sunrise to sunset
Fees and permits: No fees or permits required
Trail contact: Winnakee Land Trust, PO Box 610, Rhinebeck, NY 12572; (845) 876-4213; winnakee.org

Dog-friendly: Dogs permitted on leash
Trail surface: Dirt
Land status: Winnakee Land Trust
Nearest town: Hyde Park, New York
Other trail users: Dog walkers, joggers, cyclists; cross-country skiers in season
Maps: NatGeo TOPO! Map (USGS): Hyde Park, NY; trail map available online at winnakee.org/wp-content/uploads/2015/05/WNP_trail_map_2010b.pdf

FINDING THE TRAILHEAD
From US 9 in Hyde Park, turn on Terwilliger Road (going north, turn right; going south, turn left). Follow Terwilliger Road past Water Tower Road and turn left on Terwilliger Road Extension, following signs to the preserve. The parking area is at the end of the extension.
Trailhead GPS: N41 46.528' / W73 55.528'

WHAT TO SEE
Franklin Roosevelt was not the only landowner in Hyde Park who appreciated the value of sustainable forestry and eternal green spaces. Just down the road from the Roosevelt Farm and Forest, Franklin's friend and neighbor, Colonel Archibald Rogers, recognized young Roosevelt's interest in forest management and served as a mentor to the boy, cultivating his enthusiasm for trees until it became a lifelong passion.

Winnakee is a Native American word meaning "good land," and preservation of this land as a fertile resource became Rogers's goal. A century ago he began planting stands of white pine, many of which you see in the Winnakee Nature Preserve today—placing each seedling by hand according to the tenets of scientific forestry. Roosevelt often worked by Rogers's side, absorbing the concept of trees as a valuable, sustainable crop.

Wildflowers, ferns and plants
line the trail at Winnakee
Preserve.

The native trees and plants are truly forever wild here.

Rogers not only grew these trees but also harvested them for their lumber, carefully choosing which trees to cut down during his daily walks through these woods. The preserve's blue trail follows the remains of a logging road Rogers and his workers built through his land, allowing teams to remove the trees he marked and carry them out on wagons.

During your own hike along these trails, watch for signs of the engineering ingenuity that Rogers brought to the design of this woodland. You'll see drainage ditches and stone culverts, placed to keep spring rains and snowmelt from washing out the woods' roads. He employed a crew each summer to dig ditches to drain standing water away from the woods, preventing the development of swamps that would drown the trees' roots.

With all its utility as a sustainable forest, however, Rogers understood that his woodlands also provided natural beauty and an oasis of green space well outside the massive metropolis to the south. He built carriage roads for his family, friends, and neighbors to enjoy as they traveled through the woods; and a century later, we can make the most of his generosity by walking these carriage roads and taking the time to appreciate the preserve he created.

To further understand the impact Rogers's leadership had on the landscape of Hyde Park, visit Roosevelt Farm and Forest, part of the Home of Franklin Delano Roosevelt National Historic Site just down the road on NY 9. The trail through the Roosevelt forest is the starting point for the Hyde Park Trail.

A natural pond provides
water to woodland animals
and birds.

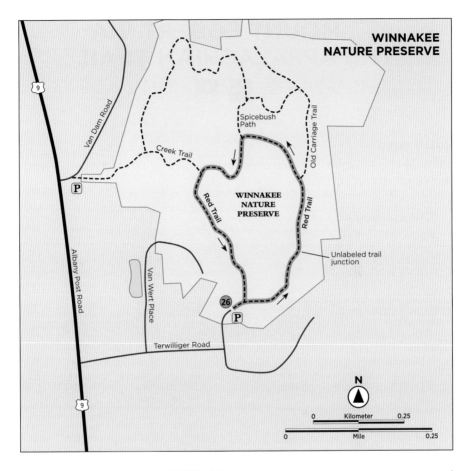

MILES AND DIRECTIONS

0.0 Start from the parking area, enter the preserve, and take the Colonel Rogers Loop Trail (red markers) to the right.

0.2 An unmarked trail goes right. Bear left on the red trail.

0.3 The Old Carriage Trail (green markers) goes right. Bear left on the red trail.

0.5 The Spicebush Path goes right. Continue left.

0.6 The Creek Trail joins here. Turn left to continue on the red trail.

0.8 Arrive back at the parking area.

27. MOUNT EGBERT VIA THE APPALACHIAN TRAIL

WHY GO?

Sample the AT and pick up a quick summit—and reward yourself with a sweeping Hudson Valley view.

THE RUNDOWN

Start: Parking area at the end of Depot Hill Road in Poughquag
Elevation gain: 167 feet
Distance: 3.0 miles out and back
Difficulty: Moderate
Hiking time: About 2.25 hours
Seasons: Year-round
Schedule: Trail open 24/7
Fees and permits: No fees or permits required
Trail contact: DEC Region 3 Office, 21 South Putt Corners Rd., New Paltz, NY 12561; (845) 256-3000; dec.ny .gov
Dog-friendly: Dogs permitted on leash
Trail surface: Dirt and last year's leaves; areas of large rock formations and slabs

Land status: Depot Hill Multiple Use Area
Nearest town: Beekman, New York
Other trail users: AT thru-hikers, trail runners
Maps: NatGeo TOPO! Map (USGS): Poughquag, NY; NatGeo Trails Illustrated Map #1508: Appalachian Trail: Delaware Water Gap to Schaghticoke Mountain; trail map available online at dec.ny.gov/ images/lands_forests_images/ mapdepothill.jpg
Special considerations: A walking stick or ski poles will help you get over and through large rock formations. Hunting is permitted here in season; timber harvesting operations in the multiple-use area also may disrupt hiking.

FINDING THE TRAILHEAD

From the Taconic State Parkway, take the NY 52 exit toward Fishkill/Carmel. Turn right onto NY 52 and drive 1.2 miles to NY 216. Turn left onto NY 216 East and continue about 5 miles to Depot Hill Road. Turn right onto Depot Hill Road and drive to the end, where there is a small parking area. Park here and walk up the dirt road with the "No Thru Traffic" sign. Watch for the Appalachian Trail white blaze on your right.
Trailhead GPS: N41 34.276' / W73 40.831'

WHAT TO SEE

Whether you've walked hundreds of miles on the Appalachian National Scenic Trail or this is your first day on the 2,190-mile footpath from Springer Mountain, Georgia,

A short hike to a gorgeous view along the Appalachian Trail is a grand day out.

The trail passes a pond just beyond the trees.

Visit an official Appalachian Trail shelter shortly before the big view.

to Mount Katahdin, Maine, this short segment to the summit of Mount Egbert is sure to please. It's meticulously maintained by the New York–New Jersey Trail Conference, including freshly painted white blazes that leave no ambiguity in directing you along the trail. You'll move through some rugged, rocky patches and past a quiet pond on your way to a satisfying view of the Hudson River Valley, a great place to stop, rest on a rock, and enjoy your packed lunch. The return trip follows the same trail—just be sure you turn north as you start back, or you may be in for a much longer trek than you planned.

It's possible that you're not familiar with the Appalachian Trail (those in the know refer to it as the AT), so let me catch you up. The AT has been in use by day hikers and long-distance trekkers since the 1920s, though a great deal of the land involved belonged to private landowners and municipalities—and some of these had never given official permission for hikers to use the land. The trail received a major boost in 1968 when it became an official part of the National Park Service. The park service set to work with the Appalachian Trail Conservancy to obtain legal permission for hikers to cross private and municipal land, creating the contiguous length managed jointly by the two organizations today.

The hike traverses part of the 267-acre Depot Hill Multiple Use Area in the towns of Beekman and Pawling, and the New York State Department of Environmental Conservation manages the area to produce forest crops and maintain habitat for a wide variety of wildlife, including white-tailed deer, wild turkey, ring-necked pheasant, fox, squirrel, rabbit, and waterfowl. Keep an eye out for small furry animals as you hike, as well as birds including red-eyed vireo, gray catbird, blue jay, wood thrush, hermit thrush, and wood-warblers during the spring and fall migrations.

Most of the elevation gain along the trail comes from the dips and rises of the terrain rather than a typical Hudson Valley climb, making this a fairly easy hike for those who enjoy bagging Hudson Valley summits. As you near the top of Mount Egbert, there's another treat in store: an official AT shelter, a well-constructed lean-to with a cleared area for picnicking, resting, and organizing gear. Here—and elsewhere on the trail—you may come across thru-hikers who have taken on the AT's entire length or section hikers who are completing the trail a few days or weeks at a time. Some will be pleased to talk with you about their experience to date; others will prefer privacy and solitude, passing you by with a brief smile and a nod. You may feel somewhat dwarfed by the enormity of the hiking adventure they have taken on, but most AT hikers won't see you that way; think of your hike as a sampler that may lead to a more comprehensive experience. Everyone starts the AT in his or her own way, and some feel the need for more once they've had a taste.

MILES AND DIRECTIONS

0.0   Start from the parking area and walk down the road with the "No Thru Traffic" sign. Watch on your right for the white blaze (next to the three blue blazes). The white blazes are for the Appalachian Trail.

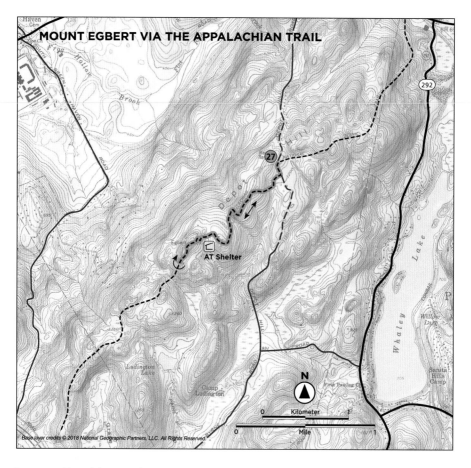

MOUNT EGBERT VIA THE APPALACHIAN TRAIL

0.1 Turn right onto the AT.

0.6 A pond appears to your left, and a large rock formation is ahead. This is the first of a series of large rock and slab formations. The AT goes over or through these.

1.2 Arrive at the AT trail shelter.

1.3 Reach the summit of Mount Egbert.

1.5 Viewpoint. When you're ready, return the way you came.

3.0 Arrive back at the parking area.

ULSTER COUNTY

When it comes to natural and geological wonders, Ulster County has it all going on. Just 90 minutes from New York City and an hour south of Albany, this county features some of the state's most fascinating landscapes and hiking opportunities—from the waterfalls and rock walls of Minnewaska State Park Preserve to the legendary Shawangunk Ridge, an internationally known destination for rock climbers.

The Gunks form the western wall of the Great Appalachian Valley, a chain of valleys that stretch from Quebec, Canada, to Alabama. The Hudson, Newburgh, and Wallkill Valleys are all part of this long lowland phenomenon, an area that once provided fairly easy passage for Native Americans traveling north to south. Later it became a trade and commerce route for European colonists, and then a railroad corridor to bring farm crops and mined materials to centers of industry.

Here you'll find an expansive valley brimming with the literal fruits of agriculture, making a visit during harvest season every bit as satisfying as a spring hike through the mountains. A nearly level hike along the Wallkill Valley Rail Trail leads through farmland planted with corn and beans, orchards loaded with ripening apples, and pastures for cattle and horses. After your hike, reward yourself with a stop at one of the many farm stands to sample local apple cider, or visit a vineyard for a flight of varietal wines made from Hudson Valley grapes.

More than 250,000 acres of designated wilderness feature 350 miles of hiking trails, leading around sky lakes, into self-chilling caves, up mountain slopes, and along ridgelines with magnificent views. No one book could cover them all, so in the pages that follow you'll find a selection of hikes that introduce you to this region's vast resources—enough to help you begin to explore on your own and find the hiking experiences that are right for you and your family.

The Shawangunk Ridge towers over the Hudson Valley on the way to Minnewaska State Park Preserve.

28. MINNEWASKA STATE PARK PRESERVE: MINNEWASKA LAKE CARRIAGE ROAD

WHY GO?
Circle one of the prettiest sky lakes in the Hudson Valley region and discover Shawangunk geology.

THE RUNDOWN

Start: Upper parking area at Lake Minnewaska, in Minnewaska State Park Preserve
Elevation gain: 128 feet
Distance: 2.0-mile loop
Difficulty: Moderate
Hiking time: About 1.5 hours
Seasons: Spring through fall
Schedule: Open daily 9 a.m.; closing time varies with season. *Note:* This trail is closed to hiking in winter when groomed for cross-country skiing. If snow conditions are not enough for skiing, the trail remains open for hiking.
Fees and permits: Entrance fee per vehicle
Trail contact: Minnewaska State Park Preserve, 5281 Route 44-55, Kerhonkson, NY 12446; (845) 255-0752; parks.ny.gov/parks/127/details.aspx

Dog-friendly: Dogs permitted on leash
Trail surface: Crushed stone
Land status: New York state park preserve
Nearest town: Kerhonkson, New York
Other trail users: Cyclists, equestrians; cross-country skiers in season
Maps: NatGeo TOPO! Map (USGS): Napanoch, NY; NatGeo Trails Illustrated Map #750: Shawangunk Mountains; New York–New Jersey Trail Conference #104: Shawangunk Trails
Special considerations: While it's highly unlikely that you will encounter them, timber rattlesnakes and copperheads make their home in the park.

FINDING THE TRAILHEAD
From the south, take I-87 north to New Paltz (exit 18) and take NY 299 West (New Paltz–Minnewaska Road) about 8 miles to the end. Turn right on NY 44/55 West and continue about 5 miles to the park preserve entrance. Once in the park, follow the signs for Lake Minnewaska and the upper parking area.
From the north, take I-87 to exit 18 and follow the directions above.
Trailhead GPS: N41 43.732' / W74 14.227'

Here's one of many viewpoints on this lovely carriage road.

WHAT TO SEE

Thank the perseverance of the State of New York for the existence of the gorgeous Minnewaska State Park Preserve, a portion of the estate owned by twin brothers Albert and Alfred Smiley. The Smileys owned this land as well as the neighboring Mohonk property, building resort hotels on each of the sites in the late 1800s—the still-popular Mohonk Mountain House and the 225-room Minnewaska Mountain House, or "Cliff House," as guests often called it. Alfred Smiley eventually managed Cliff House separately from his brother and built a second and larger hotel, Wildmere, on the Minnewaska property as well. Property manager Kenneth Phillips bought Cliff House from the Smileys in 1955, but by 1972 the aging hotel had become overwhelmingly expensive to maintain. It stood abandoned until it burned to the ground in 1978; Wildmere burned as well in 1986.

Meanwhile, as the hotels stood empty and aging, New York State had been up to its proverbial elbows in proposals from developers, as well as counterproposals from environmentalists to keep the unique scenic area from becoming another housing tract or condominium complex. The state settled the matter in 1987 by buying the property and dedicating it as a state park. In 1993 New York changed the designation to State Park Preserve under Article 20 of the Parks, Recreation and Historic Preservation law. Three years later, the Open Space Institute acquired the area now known as Sam's Point Preserve and several thousand acres adjoining Minnewaska on its western boundary. Over the next two decades, all those lands became part of Minnewaska State Park Preserve.

In 2006 a plan to build 350 luxury homes on another 2,500 adjoining acres at the base of Shawangunk Ridge met fierce opposition from residents of nearby Gardiner, who formed a community activist group called Save the Ridge to battle the plan. Years

Minnewaska Lake provides plenty of beautiful views.

of resistance finally led the developer to withdraw, making way for the sale of the parcel to the Trust for Public Land for a whopping $17 million. The Trust immediately made a gift of the land to New York State, further expanding the preserve.

The carriage road you will follow on this hike provides an introduction to the more than 35 miles of such paths in this park. You may enjoy another short hike from the parking area just past the entrance to this unit of the park: Awosting Falls, a meander of just under a mile along a creek to a dramatic waterfall. Carriage roads provide access to several delightful natural phenomena throughout the park, including Rainbow Falls, a 5.0-mile out-and-back hike from the same parking area as Awosting, with the payoff of a double waterfall (but only in spring or during very rainy summers).

MILES AND DIRECTIONS

0.0 Start from the parking area and take the crushed stone path to the lake. You'll see an interpretive sign for the Lake Minnewaska Carriage Road. Follow the red diamond-shaped markers. Turn right.

0.3 An unmarked path goes right. Bear left around the bend.

0.4 Castle Point Carriage Road goes right. Continue straight on the red diamond trail.

0.8 The Millbrook Mountain Trail continues straight here. Go left on the red diamond trail.

0.9 Reach the first great viewpoint of the lake.

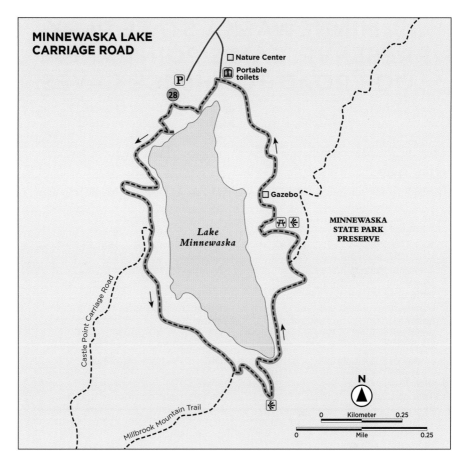

MINNEWASKA LAKE CARRIAGE ROAD

☐ Nature Center

🏛 Portable toilets

P

28

☐ Gazebo

🎌 🥾

MINNEWASKA STATE PARK PRESERVE

Lake Minnewaska

Castle Point Carriage Road

Millbrook Mountain Trail

🥾

N

| 0 | Kilometer | 0.25 |
| 0 | Mile | 0.25 |

1.0 At the end of the lake, you have a clear view of the entire area. The Millbrook Mountain footpath (red squares) starts here. Continue on the red diamond path around the lake.

1.3 An unmarked trail goes right here. Continue straight on the red diamond trail.

1.4 This is the top of the rock wall you saw from the parking area. There's a lilac grove here, a picnic area, and a spectacular view of the lake from the highest point on the trail and the site of the former Cliff House hotel.

1.5 A summer house (gazebo) offers more great views.

1.8 Come to some portable toilets. Just past these you'll find the nature center.

2.0 Arrive back at the parking area.

29. MINNEWASKA STATE PARK PRESERVE, SAM'S POINT AREA: LOOP ROAD TO THE ICE CAVES

WHY GO?

There's nothing like a naturally chilled cave on a hot summer day.

THE RUNDOWN

Start: Parking lot in Sam's Point Area of Minnewaska State Park Preserve
Elevation gain: 200 feet
Distance: 3.6 miles out and back
Difficulty: Moderate
Hiking time: About 2.5 hours
Seasons: Spring through fall
Schedule: Open daily, 9 a.m. to closing (closing time posted at preserve entrance)
Fees and permits: Entrance fee per vehicle
Trail contact: Sam's Point Area of Minnewaska State Park Preserve, 400 Sam's Point Rd., Cragsmoor, NY 12420; (845) 647-7989; parks.ny.gov/parks/127/details.aspx
Dog-friendly: Dogs permitted on leash, though hike may be too difficult for dogs.
Trail surface: Gravel and pavement to the Ice Caves entrance, then uneven stone steps that may be wet and slippery; stone and dirt cave floor, wood board walkways and wood ladders

Land status: New York state park preserve
Nearest town: Walker Valley, New York to the south; Ellenville, New York to the north
Other trail users: Hikers only
Maps: NatGeo TOPO! Map (USGS): Napanoch, NY; NatGeo Trails Illustrated Map #750: Shawangunk Mountains; New York–New Jersey Trail Conference #104: Shawangunk Trails
Special considerations: The Ice Cave Trail contains ice flows (even in summer), water, uneven rock steps, narrow crevices, low rock ceilings, dark areas, ladders and boardwalks. Use extreme caution on the trail through the cave. Wear boots with ankle support, and take your time through this trail. A walking stick may be helpful in getting down the steps. Call the office when planning a hike in spring, as the ice in the caves must melt sufficiently to allow safe passage before the trail is opened for the season.

FINDING THE TRAILHEAD

From Middletown, take NY 17 West to exit 113 for US 209. Take US 209 to NY 52 East and turn left. Continue 0.7 mile to Cragsmoor Road. Turn right onto Cragsmoor and follow it 1.5 miles. Turn right onto Sam's Point Road. The parking area is on the left, at 400 Sam's Point Rd.
Trailhead GPS: N41 40.217' / W74 21.651'

Sam's Point shares the geology of the Shawangunk Ridge.

WHAT TO SEE

This hike through a portion of Sam's Point Preserve, a unit of Minnewaska State Park Preserve, delivers a double treat—especially if you're trying to beat the heat. First, you can enjoy one of the most spectacular views available of the park and surrounding area from Sam's Point, a wide stone ledge (or a second, slightly higher ledge) that provides a 270-degree countryside panorama. Second, you can continue from the point to the Ice Caves, a labyrinth of staircases, corridors, squeezes, climbs, and wet spots that can include mounds of snow and slippery ice—even in the heat of July.

The caves here are part of the Ellenville Fault, a fracture in the earth caused by the movement of the rock walls below, forcing them to break apart. Here in Minnewaska, the resulting open fault exposed the cave passages just enough to let in some light as well as rain and snow, but not enough to heat the chasm throughout the descent to the bottom. On the day we visited, the temperature inside the cave was as much as 30 degrees lower than at the surface, making for a very welcome respite from the summer heat.

So who was Sam, and why does he have a point? The story goes that Sam, most likely a European-descended individual, managed to enrage the local Indians into chasing him through this particular area (probably in the 1700s, when tensions flared often between Native American tribes and new settlers). He reached the ledge and could either surrender—an unattractive concept that would certainly have led to his execution—or leap to his probable death. Sam chose the leap, and the fates smiled on him as he fell: The trees broke his fall, so he escaped the angry mob and probably suffered nothing worse that some scrapes and scratches. The ledge has borne his name ever since. Coming from the region that supplied us with legends including Rip Van Winkle and the Headless Horseman, the tale provides just enough truthiness to satisfy curious visitors.

The road you will follow on your way to the cave was the work of the Civilian Conservation Corps (CCC), the workforce created by President Franklin Roosevelt to train unemployed, able-bodied young men in a wide range of trades during the Great Depression of the 1930s. CCC members built roads, constructed trails, and erected facilities in national and state parks across the United States, and many of them assisted in fighting fires in the parks as well. They constructed this road to provide access to the backcountry in case of a forest fire, and this particular road became a critical asset in 2016, when 2,028 acres of the Sam's Point area burned for more than a week.

MILES AND DIRECTIONS

0.0 Start at the kiosk at the north end of the parking area and take the right-hand path toward the Ice Caves.

0.6 A large rock slab to your right offers a place to stand for a tremendous view of the surrounding area. This is the lower portion of Sam's Point.

0.7 A path to the left leads to the official Sam's Point, which is higher than the overlook you just passed.

The route through the Ice Caves has uneven stairs, aging railings, and lots of damp areas.

The view from Sam's Point seems endless on a clear day.

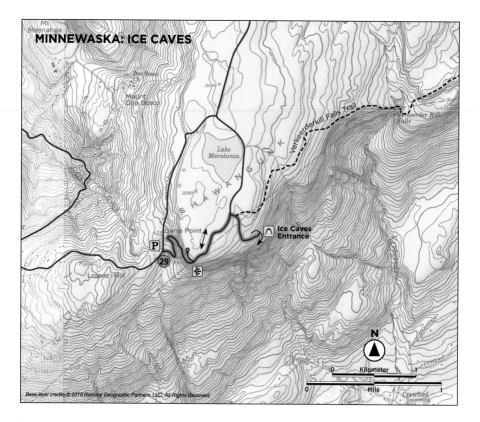

MINNEWASKA: ICE CAVES

1.1 Turn right here for the Ice Caves Trail (white blaze). The Loop Road continues straight ahead and loops around Lake Maratanza.

1.2 The Verkeerderkill Falls Trail begins here to the left. As you come around the next bend on your way to the Ice Caves, watch for another great viewpoint.

1.5 Reach the entrance to the Ice Caves. The map from here is an approximate length and path, as GPS devices don't function underground. You will go down stone steps to the bottom, then through a narrow passage, across some boardwalk, up ladders, and probably through some icy or snowy sections.

2.0 Emerge from the cave a short distance from where you went in. Return to the parking area on the trail that got you here.

3.6 Arrive back at the parking area.

30. **BLACK CREEK PRESERVE**

WHY GO?
Shady forest, vernal pools, and a dramatic suspension bridge over a dark, burbling creek—this preserve packs a lot of scenery into its 130 acres.

THE RUNDOWN

Start: Parking area on Winding Brook Acres Road
Elevation gain: 252 feet
Distance: 1.8-mile lollipop
Difficulty: Moderate
Hiking time: About 1 hour
Seasons: Year-round
Schedule: Open daily, dawn to dusk
Fees and permits: No fees or permits required; available for special events and group outings: scenichudson.org/whatyoucando/visitourparks/specialeventpermits
Trail contact: Scenic Hudson, One Civic Center Plaza, Suite 200, Poughkeepsie, NY 12601; (845) 473-4440; scenichudson.org/parks/blackcreek; e-mail: info@scenichudson.org

Dog-friendly: Dogs permitted on 6-foot leash (Please clean up and carry out any waste.)
Trail surface: Dirt path
Land status: Scenic Hudson Land Trust
Nearest town: Esopus, New York
Other trail users: Trail runners, birders, anglers; cross-country skiers in season
Maps: NatGeo TOPO! Map (USGS): Hyde Park, NY; trail map available online at scenichudson.org/sites/default/files/BlackCreek.webmap.png
Special considerations: Take precautions against poison ivy. Suspension bridge may be slippery in winter. Do not disturb seasonal woodland pools. Carry out all trash.

FINDING THE TRAILHEAD
Take I-87 to the New Paltz exit (18), and go east on NY 299 for 6 miles to the junction with US 9W. Continue north for 5.5 miles on US 9W to Winding Brooks Acres Road; turn right. The parking area is on your left, just after the turn onto Winding Brook Acres Road.
Trailhead GPS: N41 49.209' / W73 57.820'

WHAT TO SEE
Protected since 1992, Black Creek Preserve offers a network of three trails that follow the tannic acid–dyed Black Creek, wander among seasonal vernal pools, and lead to water-level views of the Hudson River. It's easy to see the entire preserve in a single hike, as the trails provide viewing access to its entire 130 acres.

Cross a suspension bridge as you begin this hike

Every unspoiled acre of the Hudson River Valley deserves protection, but this preserve offers considerable natural value beyond the river's attributes. Black Creek is spawning territory for river herring, which are saltwater fish that only migrate into freshwater tributaries like this one to spawn in spring. If you hike here in May, you may glimpse alewives, one of four species of river herring in the Hudson River, spawning on the rocky bottom of the creek. Herring may not seem like an important reason to protect a creek, but these tiny fish have a critical role in the overall food chain: They serve as food for many larger fish, birds, and animals like otters and muskrats, and human anglers use them as bait.

The thick forest provides cover, resting places, and food for migrating and year-round resident birds, including the many woodpeckers that drill holes in the dead trees throughout the preserve. Keep an eye out for the red-headed woodpecker, a stunning bird with a bright red head, white breast, blue back, and white patches on its wings. Downy, hairy, and red-bellied woodpeckers are common here as well, and you're virtually certain to hear red-eyed vireo, yellow warbler, and other common woodland birds in these woods.

Vernal pools—small, seasonal ponds that fill with water in spring but dry up in summer—are homes for small amphibians like frogs and salamanders. Keep an eye out for tiny hopping or slithering creatures as you walk the trails.

Saving land from residential or industrial development is only the first step in preserving and protecting it forever. You'll see interpretive signs here about the woolly adelgid, a nasty critter that hails from Asia and first appeared in New York in 1985. This aphid-like insect sucks the sap out of hemlock tree needles, killing the trees over time. The females lay up to 300 eggs at a time, so they multiply at an alarming rate.

Enjoy views of the Hudson in any season.

Keeping the understory healthy throughout the forest also falls to Scenic Hudson, so you will see fences that keep the resident deer from overgrazing some areas. Deer love the new shoots and small twigs on shrubs and trees, but the more they graze, the harder it is for new trees to grow and produce new leaves, seeds, nuts, and fruit. This puts all other animals in the forest at a disadvantage, as they depend on these food sources for their own sustenance.

Land stewardship—often performed by dedicated volunteers—helps make wildlife preserves like this one such delightful refuges for the human spirit as well as for animals, birds, and native plants. If you happen to run into volunteers at work, be sure to thank them for the important function they serve in this preserve.

MILES AND DIRECTIONS

0.0 Cross the driveway from the parking area, and start the trail at the archway fashioned from tree branches. The trail begins by following Black Creek. Cross a small footbridge.

0.1 Cross the suspension bridge over Black Creek, stopping to enjoy the view from above before you begin to follow the yellow plastic markers you see on trees. Enter the forest and note the predominance of young hemlock trees here. As you proceed uphill—the steepest part of the trail—you see many

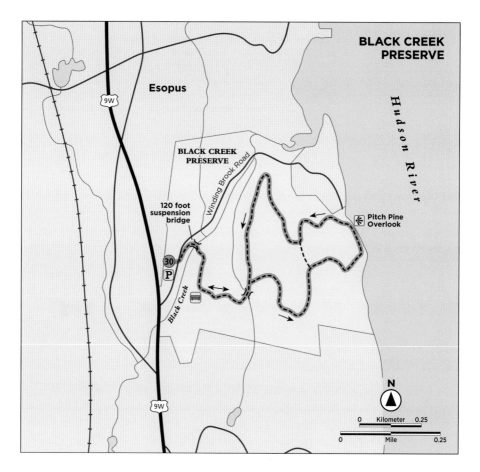

BLACK CREEK PRESERVE

Esopus

9W

BLACK CREEK
PRESERVE

Winding Brook Road

120 foot
suspension
bridge

30

P

Black Creek

Pitch Pine
Overlook

Hudson River

9W

N

| 0 | Kilometer | 0.25 |
| 0 | Mile | 0.25 |

leafy trees: American hornbeam, red maple, northern red oak, and pignut hickory.

0.2 You'll be pleased to find the bench at the top of the hill. There's an interpretive display here about trees. When you're ready, continue to follow the yellow markers.

0.3 Cross a small bridge over the creek. There's an interpretive display here about deer exclosures, fencing that keeps deer from devouring the plants that grow on the forest floor. Turn right on the red trail (you'll see red plastic markers) and continue to the vernal pools.

0.7 Turn right here on the blue trail to the Hudson River. (**Option:** You can continue straight onto the cross path between the red and blue trails and return to the parking area, but you will miss the river view.) Descend to the river on the blue trail.

0.8 Reach the Hudson River. There's usually a good breeze coming off the river here. Turn left and continue along the river for some great views.

0.9 Arrive at Pitch Pine Overlook, the best vantage point from which to enjoy the river. There's a log bench here if you'd like to pause and contemplate the view. When you're ready, the trail continues behind you. Follow the blue trail and begin a gradual ascent.

1.0 The cross trail goes straight here. Turn right on the red trail and continue through the vernal pools area. In spring look for still pools of water that may host spring peepers and other frogs. Watch on the ground for spotted salamanders and other small amphibians.

1.4 Turn right on the yellow trail; this is the trail on which you arrived. After a short ascent, the trail is mostly downhill to the suspension bridge and back to the parking area.

1.8 Arrive back at the trailhead and parking area.

31. SHAUPENEAK RIDGE: RIDGE TRAIL

WHY GO?

A cornucopia of natural features makes this little trail a local gem.

THE RUNDOWN

Start: Parking at trailhead for the White Trail, 1169 Old Post Rd. (CR 16 in Esopus) west of US 9W.

Elevation gain: 806 feet

Distance: 2.3-mile shuttle (3.4 miles out and back)

Difficulty: Moderate

Hiking time: About 1 hour as a shuttle (2 hours out and back)

Seasons: Year-round

Schedule: Open daily, dawn to dusk

Fees and permits: No fees or permits required; available for special events and group outings: scenichudson.org/whatyoucando/visitourparks/specialeventpermits

Trail contact: Scenic Hudson, One Civic Center Plaza, Suite 200, Poughkeepsie, NY 12601; (845) 473-4440; scenichudson.org/parks/shaupeneakridge

Dog-friendly: Dogs permitted on 6-foot leash (Please clean up and carry out any waste.)

Trail surface: Dirt and rock

Land status: Scenic Hudson land trust

Nearest town: Esopus, New York

Other trail users: Mountain bikers, anglers; hunters via permit during hunting season

Maps: NatGeo TOPO! Map (USGS): Hyde Park, NY; trail map available online at scenichudson.org/sites/default/files/shaupeneak-2016_webmap.jpg

Special considerations: The waterfalls are most picturesque in spring and fall after a rain. Spring turkey and fall deer hunting is permitted here; consider not hiking during hunting season, or wear bright orange for safety.

FINDING THE TRAILHEAD

From the north or south, cross the Mid-Hudson Bridge from east to west. Take US 9W north for 8.2 miles to Old Post Road; turn left. Continue 0.2 mile to the lower parking lot and the White Trailhead. GPS: N41 49.624' / W73 58.213'

If you're doing a shuttle hike, the parking area at the Red Trailhead (upper lot) is at 143 Popletown Rd. between Old Post Road and Union Center Road. Follow Old Post Road until it splits to the right. This is Popletown Road. Drive 2.5 miles on Popletown Road from the intersection of US 9W and Old Post Road, and watch for the parking area on your left. GPS: Use the street address 143 Popletown Road in Esopus / N41 50.244' / W73 59.653'.

Trailhead GPS: N41 49.624' / W73 58.213' (White Trail); N41 50.244' / W73 59.653' (Red Trail)

Take this moderate trail through rocky but pleasant woods.

WHAT TO SEE

At 892 feet at its highest point, Shaupeneak Ridge tops the Marlboro Mountains for 25 miles from Newburgh to Kingston, giving the mountains an appearance that geologists call "hogbacked." The 936.5-acre Shaupeneak Ridge Cooperative Recreation Area is owned and managed by Scenic Hudson, the largest environmental group in the Hudson Valley. With the goal of connecting people with the Hudson River, the group has preserved nearly 40,000 acres to date throughout the region.

As this is a recreation area managed jointly with the New York State Department of Environmental Conservation, you may encounter many kinds of users of this land. Hunting is permitted in season, Louisa Pond often attracts anglers, and winter may bring snowshoe hikers and cross-country skiers.

Thanks to Scenic Hudson, Shaupeneak offers 3.5 miles of well-marked trails that lead through several different habitats, from meadows filled with wildflowers in spring and summer to second-growth forest where warblers and vireos gather during the migration seasons. Oaks, hickories, hemlock and maples make up the majority of trees covering the hillsides. A creek weaves its way through the woods and tumbles down rocky ledges to form two waterfalls, including a cascade on the main (White) trail and a more delicate "curtain" falls a short distance away on a side (purple-blazed) trail that appears early in the hike.

Depending on the season, your hike will bring you to a wide view of the Hudson River to the east and, from late fall to early spring, the Catskill Mountains to the west. A fall hike will bring a prismatic and changing array of colors from early to late October, while spring and summer fill the meadows with wildflowers including common milkweed, black-eyed Susan, oxeye daisy, Queen Anne's lace, spotted knapweed, common ragweed, goldenrod, and common mullein. Keep an eye out along the trails for white and yellow sweet clover, bird's-foot trefoil, and other wildflowers.

At the same time, you're likely to see some of the invasive species that Scenic Hudson works daily to eradicate. Watch for trees with strips of bark missing; these are tree-of-heaven, an invader from China that produces hundreds of thousands of seeds each year and threatens to oust the trees that are native to New York. Removing the bark and girding sections of the tree's trunk prevents nutrients from reaching its roots, eventually killing this destructive tree.

Look for the triangle-shaped leaf of mile-a-minute vine, an aggressive creeping plant from eastern Asia and the Pacific Rim that grows at a rate so alarming that it earns its name. The plant produces colorful blue and purple berries that attract birds, squirrels, and chipmunks; the seeds come out in their droppings, dispersing wherever the animals and birds go next. With funding from New York State's Environmental Protection Fund, Scenic Hudson has been working with the local community to slow the spread of this plant. Efforts have included coordinated removals on seven properties, community focused education, and the introduction of insect predators to reduce the population of mile-a-minute over time.

The ridge view reveals an unusual angle of the Hudson Valley.

This curtain falls appears on the purple-blazed side trail.

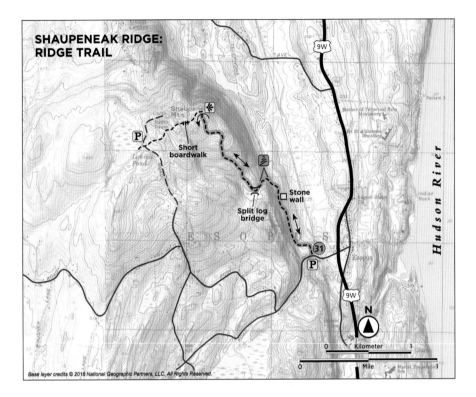

MILES AND DIRECTIONS

0.0 Start from the lower parking area and follow the White Trail. (There is only one trailhead here.)

0.5 Pass a stone wall.

0.7 The Purple Trail goes right. Take this trail to the waterfalls. In a few moments you'll see the falls—a curtain waterfall over moss-covered rocks. When you're ready, return to the main trail by following the Purple Trail back the way you came. This all added about 0.1 mile to your hike.

0.8 Here's a second waterfall just off the White Trail. This is a smaller but more dramatic cascade.

0.9 Cross the creek on a split-log bridge.

1.7 Reach the top of the ridge. There's a nice view of the Hudson River and the surrounding hills. (**Option:** If you're doing an out-and-back hike, this is your turnaround point. Return the way you came on the White Trail for a total hike of 3.4 miles.) If you have a second car parked at the Red Trailhead, turn left here and continue on the Red Trail.

1.9 Come to a short wooden boardwalk over a wet area.

2.3 Arrive at the Red Trailhead and your second vehicle.

32. WALLKILL VALLEY RAIL TRAIL: NEW PALTZ TO ROSENDALE

WHY GO?
A walk in the woods to an ingeniously repurposed train trestle and fabulous valley views.

THE RUNDOWN

Start: Parking/fishing access area on Springtown Road at Cereus Way, outside New Paltz
Elevation gain: 242 feet
Distance: 3.4-mile shuttle (6.8 miles out and back)
Difficulty: Easy
Hiking time: 2.5 hours as a shuttle
Seasons: Year-round
Schedule: Open daily, dawn to dusk
Fees and permits: No fees or permits required
Trail contact: Wallkill Valley Rail Trail Association, PO Box 1048, New Paltz, NY 12561; wvrta.org
Dog-friendly: Dogs permitted on leash

Trail surface: Packed dirt, some mowed grass areas
Land status: Wallkill Valley Rail Trail Association
Nearest town: New Paltz, New York; Rosendale, New York
Other trail users: Cyclists, equestrians, joggers, trail runners; cross-country skiers in season
Maps: NatGeo TOPO! Map (USGS): Rosendale, NY; NatGeo Trails Illustrated Map #750: Shawangunk Mountains; trail map available online at wvrta.org/enjoying-the-trail/map/
Special considerations: In-town sections of this trail can be heavily used on weekends. Consider a weekday hike.

FINDING THE TRAILHEAD

From New Paltz, take NY 299 West to Springtown Road; turn right on Springtown. Continue 4.1 miles to the parking area for fishing access to the Wallkill River (GPS: N41 48.133' / W74 05.116'). Park here and cross Springtown Road on foot to Cereus Way, where you have access to the Wallkill Valley Rail Trail.

For the shuttle, park your destination car in the lot on Binnewater Drive in Rosendale, just off NY 213. From New Paltz, drive north on Springtown Road to the junction with NY 213 in Rosendale. Turn left on NY 213 (Main Street) and watch for the turn onto CR 7/Binnewater Drive. Turn right on Binnewater and continue to the parking area, which will be on your left. GPS: N41 50.893' / W74 05.272'
Trailhead GPS: N41 48.183' / W74 05.215'

WHAT TO SEE

If you saw the words "rail trail" in the title of this hike and assumed this would be just another flat, dog-walking and jogging path for local residents, let me assure you that this section of the Wallkill Valley Rail Trail is something truly special. This path leads through farmland, pastures, and unusual rock formations until it reaches the Rosendale Trestle, a 940-foot-long, 150-foot high railroad bridge that has been reimagined for foot and bicycle traffic.

The Wallkill Valley Rail Trail sprang from the inspiration of a group of volunteers who, back in 1983, saw an opportunity to turn the disused railroad bed into an asset the entire region could enjoy. They persevered for years to wrangle the many different companies, organizations, and agencies involved until, finally, they had the necessary permissions to begin clearing the tracks and converting the corridor into a natural environment. The trail opened in 1991, but its development has continued in the ensuing decades as the Wallkill Valley Rail Trail Association carries out its plans to lengthen, expand, and improve its resources.

The opening of the refurbished Rosendale Trestle represents one of the association's most laudable accomplishments. Originally built in 1872, the trestle stood as the highest

See where the railroad broke through rock formations to form a straightaway.

A recent renovation of the Rosendale Trestle produced a pedestrian passage over the Wallkill River.

The Rosendale Trestle has become a favorite spot for people throughout the Wallkill Valley.

span bridge in the United States, and it served until the Wallkill Valley Railroad took its last run in 1977. Turning the bridge into a destination for hikers, runners, cyclists, and sightseers required a fundraising campaign to raise the $1.5 million required, but the association partnered with the Wallkill Valley Land Trust, and their efforts succeeded. The trestle reopened in 2013 and instantly made a hit with residents and visitors.

The trestle crosses Rondout Creek in the town of Rosendale, and it provides an unprecedented view of the creek's own forest-covered valley to the west, with an equally impressive view of downtown Rosendale in the opposite direction. At one end, Joppenbergh Mountain towers over the continued trail; the other end skims the tops of tulip trees for a serendipitous display of blooms if you happen to visit in mid-May.

The Rosendale Trestle provides the grand finale for an entirely satisfying hike that begins on Springtown Road in New Paltz. We chose this particular starting place because of its easy parking and trail access, and because we wanted to explore the newest section of the rail trail. The section described here is part of the recent 11.5-mile extension of the trail from New Paltz through the town of Ulster, bringing the trail's total length to 22 miles.

Whether you hike this section or a longer one, keep in mind that there's much more to see on this rail trail than the trestle. You'll cross a section of the venerable Mohonk Preserve via the Lime Kiln Trail, just south of the mountain road. A trail up to Joppenbergh Mountain starts behind Main Street in Rosendale, and then a cave-like limestone mine opening emits blasts of frigid air even on the hottest days. In between you'll share the trail with chipmunks, squirrels, rabbits, and white-tailed deer, and you're almost certain to see blue jays scouting for food and northern cardinals swooping from tree to tree. The trail may be flat, but its attractions are many—so put away your smartphone and keep your eyes open.

MILES AND DIRECTIONS

0.0 Start from the parking area, cross Springtown Road, and proceed to your right to Cereus Way. The gravel rail trail appears to your right.

0.3 Eddie Lane crosses the trail. Continue straight.

0.5 A farm lane crosses the trail. There's a nice view to your left of the nearest ridges of the Shawangunks. Watch for occasional remnants of the railroad tracks embedded in the ground.

1.1 A long private driveway crosses the trail.

1.2 In this rock face you can see the drill cuts made by workers who conducted the blasting operations to clear the way for track construction.

1.3 A bridge crosses a stream and a road here.

1.4 In the clearing to your left, you'll see At the Rail Trail Café, which is open on weekends in season. There's a bike rental shop here as well.

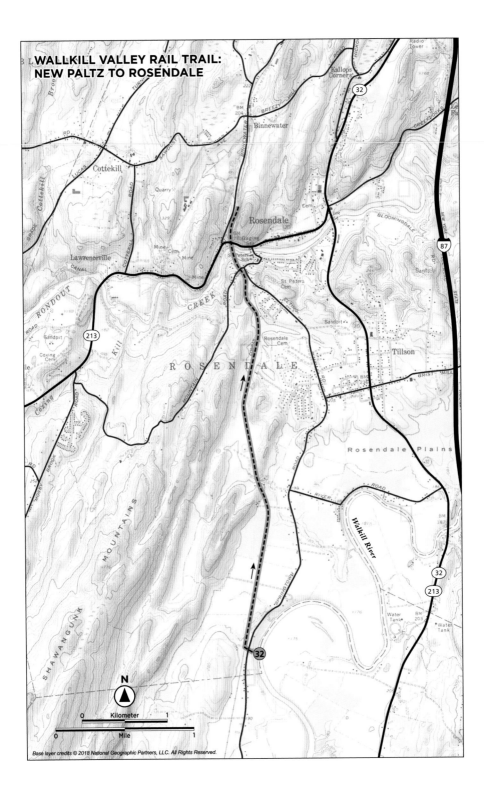

WALLKILL VALLEY RAIL TRAIL:
NEW PALTZ TO ROSENDALE

N

0   Kilometer   1

0   Mile   1

Base layer credits © 2018 National Geographic Partners, LLC. All Rights Reserved.

2.0 A neighborhood access trail enters from the right. You'll see a lot of these in the next mile or so. As the trail begins to follow a stream on your left, you're adjacent to the lands of Mohonk Preserve.

2.6 Here's an interpretive sign for the Grant's Ledges Pocket Park.

2.9 Cross the road in the crosswalk. In a moment you've reached the Rosendale Trestle Bridge. If it's May, look right to see if the massive tulip tree is in bloom.

3.1 The trestle bridge ends. You can see a trail to your right, but it's not the official trail to Joppenbergh Mountain. Do not take this trail up—it has many loose gravel sections and is not safe. The trail to the top starts and returns in the parking area behind Main Street in the town of Rosendale. Continue straight to stay on the rail trail.

3.3 Take this turn to the left to the destination parking area.

3.4 Arrive at your shuttle vehicle.

33. UPPER VERNOOY KILL FALLS TRAIL

WHY GO?

Meander through deep woods to this wedding-cake falls on the outskirts of Catskill Park.

THE RUNDOWN

Start: End of Trails End Way, at the yellow gate with the stop sign
Elevation gain: 348 feet
Distance: 2.0 miles out and back
Difficulty: Easy
Hiking time: About 1 hour
Seasons: Spring and fall
Schedule: Open daily, dawn to dusk
Fees and permits: No fees or permits required
Trail contact: NYSDEC Region 3, 21 South Putt Corners Rd., New Paltz, NY 12561; (845) 256-3064; dec.ny .gov/lands/75346.html
Dog-friendly: Dogs permitted on leash

Trail surface: Dirt path with many rocks and roots
Land status: New York State Department of Environmental Conservation (NYSDEC)
Nearest town: Ellenville, New York
Other trail users: Horseback riders; snowmobilers in season
Maps: NatGeo TOPO! Map (USGS): Napanoch, NY; NatGeo Trails Illustrated Map #750: Shawangunk Mountains; trail map available online at alltrails.com/explore/trail/us/new-york/vernooy-falls-trail

FINDING THE TRAILHEAD

From Ellenville, take US 209 North to CR 3 (Samsonville Road). Turn left onto CR 3 and in 3.4 miles bear left onto Upper Cherry Town Road. Continue on Upper Cherry Town Road (past the parking area on this road) until it ends at Trails End Way. Turn left and drive on Trails End Way until it becomes a dirt road; continue on the dirt road until it ends at a parking area. You will see a yellow gate with a stop sign. This is the trailhead.
Trailhead GPS: N41 53.050' / W74 21.635'

WHAT TO SEE

Pick a warm spring day and walk this fairly easy trail to a many-faceted waterfall that probably receives far less than its fair share of visitors. The rocky path through the lush Sundown Wild Forest, a preserve tended by the New York State Department of Environmental Conservation, seems not as well-worn as many others we hiked for this book—perhaps because the path begins in a wilderness area far behind a sparse housing

Upper Vernooy Kill flows through this wilderness area.

development. You need to pay attention while you're driving here, as lots of side roads and surface changes can confuse you and send you off in the wrong direction. Give it a try, however, because this waterfall and the surrounding preserve are well worth the trouble.

The trail through these woods is a multiuse path, so you may run into people on horseback in spring and summer or on snowmobiles in winter. It's part of an 11.2-mile loop that begins in the tiny town of Rochester (not to be confused with the thriving metropolis of the same name on the shores of Lake Ontario) and passes through Balsam Swamp and over Vernooy Kill. (You will only see a mile of that length on this hike.) Like most trails in the Catskills, this one features many embedded rocks and some large boulders. You may be distracted by small furry animals, a white-tailed deer or two, and the occasional patch of wildflowers, so don't forget to watch your step.

The falls drop down a series of ledges stacked one on top of the other, spreading out toward the base to create the wedding-cake effect. One of these layers flows right under a bridge over Vernooy Kill ("kill" is the Dutch word for stream), and the widely spaced boards on the bridge deck allow you to see the falls flowing directly beneath your feet.

The verdant woodland thrives along the river's edge.

Upper Vernooy Kill Falls is one of the prettiest in the Hudson Valley.

A quick walk along the kill brings you to the end of the falls' many short drops for an excellent view of the entire water feature from the bottom.

Don't miss the stone wall along the stream, the last remains of the Vernooy Mill complex that harnessed the power of the kill and its falls from the early 1700s until 1809. Here settler Cornelius Vernooy took over the gristmill built by his father sometime around 1702 and ground grain into flour for other colonists in the area. Originally arriving as Dutch immigrants, the Vernooys were fruitful and multiplied here on the edge of the Catskills, settling in Rochester, Marbletown, and Kingston and leaving behind many records of their financial and legal transactions. If you'd like to know more about the Vernooy mill days, Historic Huguenot Street—a National Historic Landmark district in New Paltz—preserves a number of stone houses from the early eighteenth century, as well as interpretive materials to help you imagine what the life of the Vernooys (and many other families) may have been like.

MILES AND DIRECTIONS

0.0 Start from the parking area at the end of Trails End Road, and take the reddish-orange marked path around the yellow gate with the stop sign. Cross a footbridge and follow the "Snowmobile Trail" markers. You can see

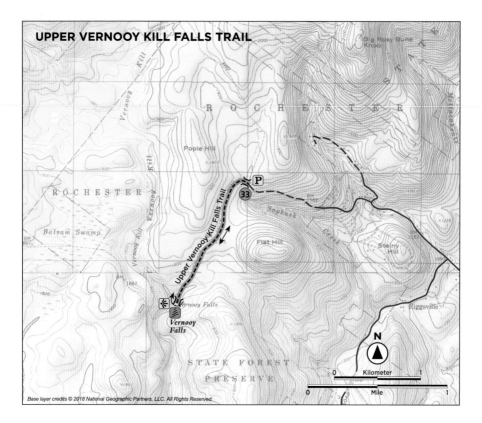

UPPER VERNOOY KILL FALLS TRAIL

bright-blue trail markers and aqua blazes for the Long Trail on this path as well.

0.6 Cross through a wet area on the path. There's a second wet area coming up, just as you begin to hear the falls.

1.0 The trail goes right and left. Go left toward the falls. In a moment, reach a clearing where you'll see the trail registry. The bridge over the falls is in sight; walk out onto the bridge to view the falls. If you like, continue along the kill another 50 feet or so for more views of the falls. When you're ready, return on the path you followed to get here.

2.0 Arrive back at the parking area.

COLUMBIA AND GREENE COUNTIES

If you're looking for a getaway into the rural countryside, Columbia County may provide just the atmosphere and landscape your soul craves. Here you will find acre after acre of farmland with rows of corn and beans in perfect symmetry, and pastures dotted with dairy cattle, sheep, goats, and occasional llamas. Inviting towns with rich, textured pasts welcome you to stop and stay in their historic inns, while estates left behind by the wealthy and talented tell stories of art, culture, and early American politics. You may be so captivated that your initial visit will be the first of many.

On the west side of the Hudson River, Greene County's hills rise until they reach Hunter Mountain, which peaks at 4,040 feet—the second-highest mountain in the Catskills (at 4,180 feet, Slide Mountain in Ulster County beats Hunter). You don't need to climb the highest mountain to enjoy the undulating green spectacle that is the Catskills, however; this region provides easily accessed viewpoints along many of their trails, including the ones in this book.

Here at higher altitudes, you'll find a change in the trees and birds you'll see along the trails, especially if you normally live closer to sea level. Maple and beech trees provide welcome shade at lower elevations with their wide, flat leaves. Oak trees drop their acorns along paths for red squirrels and eastern chipmunks to find. Higher up in the mountains, balsam fir fills the air with its earthy, spicy scent; red spruce provides cones for seed-eating birds to snap open; and paper birch trees allow birds and small animals to peel back the loose, bright white bark to find insects beneath it.

Sprinkled among these formidable peaks is a selection of small towns, offering visitors places to eat, replace your boot laces, buy extra snacks, and poke through art galleries and shops. Sparsely populated, the Catskills provide the relative quiet and solitude you may seek in your getaway from the big city—and all the natural sights and sounds you need to refresh your senses.

Fall is an especially good time to visit the Catskill and Taconic Mountains.

34. TACONIC STATE PARK: COPAKE FALLS MINE AREA AND BASH BISH FALLS

WHY GO?

Walk from the remains of an 1800s ironworks in New York to a glorious waterfall in Massachusetts.

THE RUNDOWN

Start: Main parking area for the Copake Falls developed area in Taconic State Park
Elevation gain: 392 feet
Distance: 2.6 miles out and back in two directions
Difficulty: Moderate
Hiking time: About 1.5 hours
Season: Spring through fall
Schedule: Trails open daily, dawn to dusk
Fees and permits: Parking fee from Memorial Day to Labor Day
Trail contacts: Taconic State Park, Route 344, Copake Falls, NY 12517; (518) 329-3993; http://nysparks.com/parks/83/details.aspx

Dog-friendly: Dogs permitted on trails on leash; dogs not permitted in historic buildings
Trail surface: Dirt and woodland detritus to ironworks; path constructed in stone to falls
Land status: New York state park
Nearest town: Copake, New York
Other trail users: Joggers, families with children
Maps: NatGeo TOPO! Map (USGS): Copake, NY; NatGeo Trails Illustrated Map #1509: Appalachian Trail, Schaghticoke Mountain to East Mountain; trail map available online at nysparks.com/parks/83/maps.aspx

FINDING THE TRAILHEAD

From Albany, take I-90 East to exit B2 for the Taconic State Parkway toward NY 295. Continue 10.7 miles on the parkway to CR 21 and NY 22. Turn left onto CR 21 and drive 5.5 miles to NY 22; bear right. In about 8 miles, turn left onto NY 344 West. Turn right into Taconic State Park and watch for the parking area on your left.
Trailhead GPS: N42 07.013' / W73 30.472'

WHAT TO SEE

This hike has two branches in opposite directions, with parking more or less at the midpoint between the two destinations. You may want to do just one of these two hikes during your visit, depending on the amount of time you have available. Both are worthwhile

hikes, with the Copake Iron Works a little less traveled than the very popular hike to Bash Bish Falls.

From its opening in 1845 to its gradual shutdown between 1903 and 1908, Copake Mine Iron Works produced some 4,000 tons of cast iron every year. Oddly enough, even though the mine meant big business in this corner of the Taconic Mountains—with its own railroad stop to transport the iron to industries across the country—very little is known about the business itself. We do know that the ironworks' founder, Lemuel Pomeroy, had worked in the iron trades since he was a young man, giving up college and dreams of becoming an attorney when he discovered an unexpected passion for iron-working. His holding company, Lemuel Pomeroy & Sons of Pittsfield, Massachusetts, ran the Livingston furnace in Ancram for ten years before Pomeroy and his sons discovered the site at Copake Falls. This spot afforded them water power and a strong bed of iron ore, two critical components for a successful operation.

The furnace blasted its first cast iron in 1846, and by 1847 the Copake Iron Company needed to add a forge "for the purpose of converting the cast-iron into wrought-iron, and preparing it for use in the manufacture of car-axles and gun-barrels," according to historian Captain Franklin Ellis in 1878.[1] Soon roads were built, crews felled acres of trees to turn them into charcoal to keep the furnace running, and the railroad was rerouted to move the iron more efficiently than the horse-drawn carts the ironworks employed in its early years.

Here you can see the charcoal blast furnace constructed in 1872, the office and brick powder storage building, the brick engine house, a scattering of workers' homes, and

---

1   GenNet, retrieved October 15, 2015; usgennet.org/usa/ny/county/columbia/copake/iron_works.htm

Structures from the iron mining era remain, along with an open-air museum.

one larger home in the Greek Revival style. The Church of St. John in the Wilderness is located here as well.

Your hike to the ironworks takes you along the banks of Bash Bish Brook, through an area that was once a center of industrial activity. Interpretive signs along the way help you make sense of the hulking shells of structures left behind when the ironworks shut down in the early 1900s, and an excellent museum tells the story about iron as an important commodity to New York's growth and prosperity.

The hike to Bash Bish Falls leads up a well-developed trail and across the state line into Massachusetts. The waterfall—split by a rocky outcropping in the middle of the river—is a must-see destination for people traveling through the Taconic Mountains, an area not especially well known to people who do not live nearby. Choose a hiking day in spring or early summer, when the cascade is at its fiercest.

MILES AND DIRECTIONS

0.0   Start at the parking area. You can see trailheads here for Copake Iron Works and Bash Bish Falls. The trail to the ironworks begins west of the parking area; follow the sign to Trail to Iron Works. Walk through the additional parking area to the bridge, and cross the river.

0.1   Across the bridge on the right is a "Trail to Iron Works" sign.

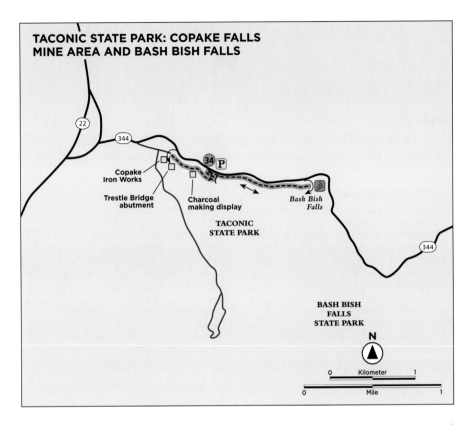

TACONIC STATE PARK: COPAKE FALLS MINE AREA AND BASH BISH FALLS

22

344

34 P

Copake Iron Works

Trestle Bridge abutment

Charcoal making display

Bash Bish Falls

TACONIC STATE PARK

BASH BISH FALLS STATE PARK

344

N

Kilometer

Mile

0.2 Come to an interpretive sign about making charcoal. The trail follows Bash Bish Brook on your right and passes the very pretty Day Pond on the left.

0.4 Reach the trestle bridge abutment.

0.5 Arrive at the ironworks. Here you can explore the forge area, the museum, and the furnace. When you are ready, take the same trail back to the parking area. (Note that the trail signs now say "Bash Bish Falls.")

1.0 Cross the parking area to the Bash Bish Falls trailhead and follow the light blue blazes.

1.1 Pass the "No Swimming" sign; the trail begins to climb.

1.6 Reach the New York–Massachusetts border and enter Bash Bish Falls State Park.

1.8 Reach the overlook for Bash Bish Falls. From here, stairs go down to a natural rock viewing platform at the base of the falls. When you are ready, return the way you came (it's all downhill in this direction).

2.6 Arrive back at the parking area.

35. **BEEBE HILL FIRE TOWER**

WHY GO?

Hike to a lonely tower to gaze across the Catskill and Taconic Mountains, as forest rangers did in the early days of fire detection.

THE RUNDOWN

Start: Parking area on Osmer Road, off NY 22 north of Austerlitz
Elevation gain: 488 feet
Distance: 2.0-mile loop
Difficulty: Moderate
Hiking time: About 1.5 hours
Seasons: Spring through fall
Schedule: Open daily, dawn to dusk
Fees and permits: No fees or permits required
Trail contact: NYSDEC Region 4, 1130 North Westcott Rd., Schenectady, NY 12306; (518) 357-2068; dec.ny.gov

Dog-friendly: Dogs permitted on leash
Trail surface: Dirt and rock, woodland path
Land status: New York State Department of Environmental Conservation (NYSDEC)
Nearest town: Austerlitz, New York
Other trail users: Mountain bikers
Maps: NatGeo TOPO! Map (USGS): State Line, NY; trail map available online at dec.ny.gov/lands/66468.html

FINDING THE TRAILHEAD

From Austerlitz, take NY 22 North to the junction with Osmer Road. Bear left on Osmer and continue 1.8 miles to the parking area, just past Barrett Pond on your left.
Trailhead GPS: N42 20.338' / W73 28.421'

WHAT TO SEE

Back in 1928, Alander Mountain in the Berkshires—just over the border from here in Massachusetts—was judged to be a good place for a forest ranger to watch the state's forests for the wisps of smoke that could signal a forest fire. Five years later, however, the state's forest management decided that Washburn Mountain in Columbia County offered a better vantage point. The tower was moved to that mountain—which must have required some disassembly of the 60-foot structure—and remained there for thirty-one years. In 1964 the tower was moved one more time to Beebe Hill, where it stands today.

No one uses this tower to look for fires anymore, as technology offers a safer and less lonely way to survey the miles of forest in every direction. Today the tower is an attraction for hikers who otherwise might never discover this entirely respectable mountain,

Take the fire road up to
the Beebe Hill Fire Tower.

FIRE LOOKOUTS: SOLITUDE AND SMOKE

In the early 1900s, before computer technology could predict fires in wilderness areas and cameras, scout planes, and drones could find them, people known as fire lookouts climbed to the top of fire towers and spent their days and nights watching for billowing smoke across vast wooded areas. This practice began long before Congress created the USDA Forest Service in 1905, but the forestry department stepped up production of fire towers in the 1910s and 1920s.

Why the concern? Everyone in the forestry and lumber businesses knew what kind of destruction a fire could cause. They had seen the Big Blowup, a rapidly spreading blaze in 1910 that consumed 3 million acres in Washington, Idaho, and Montana—possibly still the largest single forest fire ever recorded. Losing that kind of acreage would mean no lumber to build buildings, no pulp for creating paper, and all kinds of other shortages. For those who see the intrinsic value of preserving millions of acres of forested land as natural space, the loss of so much forest would be devastating.

Before fire towers, fire lookouts climbed trees to watch for smoke, or they hiked to the highest peaks, erected a tent, and watched from there. These uncomfortable options became impractical over time, and fire towers provided a much more desirable and effective solution. Fire lookouts spent countless hours alone at the top of the tower, scanning the horizon for approaching lightning storms or watching for telltale plumes of smoke. It took a certain kind of person to endure this—one who craved time alone for pursuits including painting, writing, photography, bird and wildlife watching, even knitting.

Today the forest service still operates dozens of fire towers as a first line of defense in particularly at-risk areas. "It seems human eyes and intelligence can still do things that drones, satellites, and infrared cameras cannot," Rory Carroll wrote in *The Guardian* during his visit to the Stonewall fire lookout in Montana. He noted that the people who staff these lookouts are known affectionately as "freaks on the peaks."[1]

---

1 "Freaks on the Peaks: The Lonely Lives of the Last Remaining Fire Lookouts." *The Guardian*. Retrieved from theguardian.com/us-news/2016/aug/30/us-national-parks-fire-lookout-forest-wildfire?CMP=share_btn_fb.

the wealth of warblers and vireos that use the adjoining Barrett Pond as a stopping place during the spring migration, or the artifacts of ranger life at the top of the hill.

Today Beebe Hill offers an energetic hike up to its 1,786-foot summit and an opportunity to climb the tower—if nine flights of stairs and tiny viewing spaces do not pose problems for you. Here you also will find the observer's cabin, as well as a campers' lean-to a short distance down the trail.

You may encounter a range of visitors to Beebe Hill State Forest, including anglers who come to enjoy the 6.5-acre pond and its selection of fish species including largemouth bass, bluegill, rock bass, and yellow perch; mountain bikers, equestrians on the fire road; cross-country skiers in winter; hunters and trappers in season; birders; and picnickers. While this forest and the neighboring Harvey Mountain State Forest are protected

The only way to see the view is to climb to the top of the tower.

A wooden shelter provides a stopping place on your way down the woodland trail.

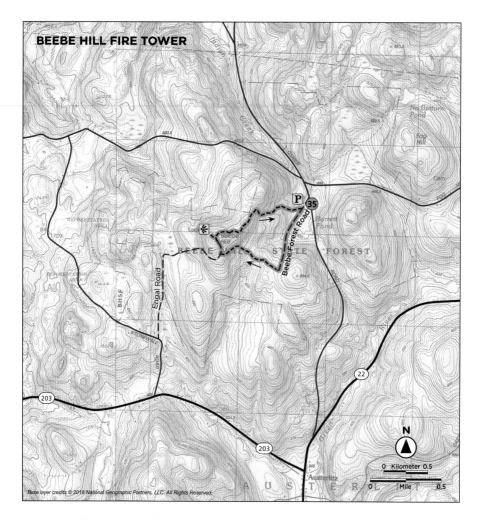

and managed for the wildlife that live or pass through here, these two woods also provide timber for industrial use. You may glimpse timber harvest operations on your hiking day.

In New York, nineteen fire towers operated in the Catskill region, and fire lookouts watched from fifty-two towers in the Adirondacks. Although New York State phased out the use of fire towers in the 1980s and closed the last ones in the 1990s, many still stand today, and volunteers across the state have worked to restore several of them. If you'd like to see more of these towers, you don't have far to travel. You can find more historic towers in the Catskills at Balsam Lake Mountain, Red Hill, Hunter Mountain, Grafton Lakes State Park, Tremper Mountain, Overlook Mountain, and at Mount Utsayantha Mountaintop Park.

MILES AND DIRECTIONS

0.0 Start at the parking area and take the fire road up the hill. Go around the gate to the left of the parking area, next to Barrett Pond. You may see orange arrows and other graphics painted on the ground as you walk.

0.5 At the top of a rise and around the corner, the Lower Horse Trail Loop joins from the left. Continue straight.

1.0 The fire road forms a T intersection with another road. The orange arrows point left, but go right to the fire tower.

1.1 Come to the observer's cabin. In about 100 feet there's a small, boarded-up building, then the fire tower. There's no view from the ground, so you need to climb the fire tower. It's nine flights of stairs to the top. When you're ready, come down and take the trail through the woods, following the round red markers.

1.3 A pond appears on your right. Shortly after, the trail forms a Y. You can see a lean-to through the trees. Visit it if you like, then return to the main trail (left at the Y junction).

1.7 Reach a stone wall.

1.8 Cross a bridge over a stream.

1.9 Reach the trail registry.

2.0 Cross a split-log bridge over a stream, and arrive back at the parking area.

36. NORTH-SOUTH LAKE PARK: CATSKILL ESCARPMENT LOOP

WHY GO?

There's no better way to take in the vibrant Catskill Mountains scenery than on this trail, where you will see the area from many angles.

THE RUNDOWN

Start: Parking area on Scutt Road just before entrance to North-South Lake Campground
Elevation gain: 509 feet
Distance: 4.9-mile lollipop
Difficulty: Strenuous
Hiking time: About 4 hours
Seasons: Spring through fall
Schedule: Trail open 24/7
Fees and permits: Day-use fee at entrance for parking during peak seasons; no fee to hike this trail
Trail contacts: North-South Lake Campground, CR 18, Haines Falls, NY 12436; (518) 357-2289 or (518) 589-5058; dec.ny.gov/outdoor/24487.html
Dog-friendly: Dogs permitted on leash (You may be asked to provide proof of a valid rabies inoculation at the campground entrance.)

Trail surface: Dirt and rock, some scrambling up large rocks
Land status: NYS Department of Environmental Conservation
Nearest town: Haines Falls, New York
Other trail users: Mountain bikers; equestrians on the yellow-blazed sections
Maps: NatGeo TOPO! Map (USGS): Kaaterskill Clove; NatGeo Trails Illustrated Map #755: Catskill Park; trail map available online at catskillmountaineer.com/hiking-escarpment-SW.html
Special considerations: Black bears live in the Catskills, and they are frequently spotted in the vicinity of this trail. Before you undertake this hike, make sure you know what to do if you come across a bear in the woods. (See "Critters" in this book's introduction.)

FINDING THE TRAILHEAD

From the south, take I-87 North to exit 20 at Saugerties. Follow NY 32 North for approximately 6 miles to NY 32A to NY 23A West. Stay on NY 23A to the village of Haines Falls. Take your first right onto CR 18. The campground entrance is at the end of the road in 2 miles.

From the north, take I-87 South to exit 21 at Catskill. Turn left onto NY 23 East and continue to US 9W South. Follow US 9W through Catskill to NY 23A. Follow 23A West to Haines Falls. Make the first right turn in Haines Falls onto CR18. The campground entrance is at the end of the road in 2 miles.

Trailhead GPS: N42 12.045' / W74 03.511'

WHAT TO SEE

If you've heard about the Catskills but never visited, or if you've wondered about the best places to see the most sweeping views of the Catskill Mountains in their full glory—especially in fall—then this solid hiking experience is for you. Make a day of it, and explore all the side trails that lead to slices of the region's history in hospitality and tourism, and from which you can see the views that inspired the first truly American style and philosophy of fine art: the Hudson River School of landscape painting.

Three major resorts served guests during "season" here from the mid-1800s into the mid-1900s: Kaaterskill Hotel, Laurel House, and the venerable Catskill Mountain House. These hotels drew the wealthiest city dwellers from all over the state and beyond, including a core group of artists of a uniquely American approach to painting known as the Hudson River School. Artists, including Thomas Cole, came to the Catskill Mountain House to paint the extraordinary view from its front lawn—Cole's famous *A View of the Two Lakes and Mountain House, Catskill Mountains, Morning* was one result. Authors Washington Irving, James Fenimore Cooper, and John Bartram all referred to this resort in their writings, and three US presidents—Ulysses Grant, Chester Arthur, and Theodore Roosevelt—came here for a respite from the pressures of the office.

Your hike begins in the parking area at North-South Lake Campground, a stunningly beautiful area in its own right. From the Scutt Road parking area, walk up Scutt Road (it's easier and less annoying than the root-crossed blue-blazed trail at this point, though they both lead to the main trailhead) and then follow the trail marked with blue DEC markers. Stay on the blue-blazed trail for most of this hike, leaving it to enhance your experience with side trails to magnificent Kaaterskill Falls, one of New York State's most

Take the bridge to see Kaaterskill Falls from the top.

Kaaterskill Falls drops 264 feet from this point— and this is just the top half of the falls.

dramatic waterfalls; and to the sites of the former Kaaterskill Hotel and Catskill Mountain House, two of the most popular mountain retreats for the wealthy when the Catskills provided a respite from the intense heat and foul air of a New York City summer.

After Layman's Monument, scramble up to a series of narrow ledges that provide stunning views of the mountains, distant ravines and waterfalls, and valleys that make the Catskills such a popular place to hike. Watch your step as you traverse these slender overlooks; if you want to enjoy the view for a bit before you continue, stop walking while you do so.

UNCOMMON VALOR REMEMBERED

Many of the landmarks that once dotted this land now remain only as foundations and memories, so Layman's Monument stands out as a place you may want to linger. This stone obelisk commemorates the courage of 25-year-old firefighter Frank Layman, who died here on August 10, 1900, when a forest fire engulfed him before he could jump off the ledge to escape. The monument stands where his comrades found him once the fire was under control, making this a particularly poignant place to pause as you walk this trail through the landscape he gave his life to save.

When you're not faced with one wide, entrancing view of the area after another, your hike takes you through forested lands dominated by red maple, beech, and oak trees, with some stands of paper birch and a scattering of hemlocks. The fragrant woods attract a wide variety of birds and small furry animals, as well as white-tailed deer and the occasional black bear. Keep your eyes and ears open for species you may not normally see in your own backyard, including the potential for deer, porcupine, and fisher, a weasel-like animal reintroduced in the Catskills in the early 1900s after hunters and trappers extirpated them. Some lucky hikers have the chance to spot a bobcat, an animal of minimal danger to humans.

MILES AND DIRECTIONS

0.0 Start from the Scutt Road parking area and walk south on Scutt Road.

0.4 Turn left and walk past the barrier.

0.5 At the trailhead, turn right. Follow the trail with blue trail markers. Immediately cross a bridge over a creek.

After some scrambling and lots of uphill, the view makes it all worthwhile.

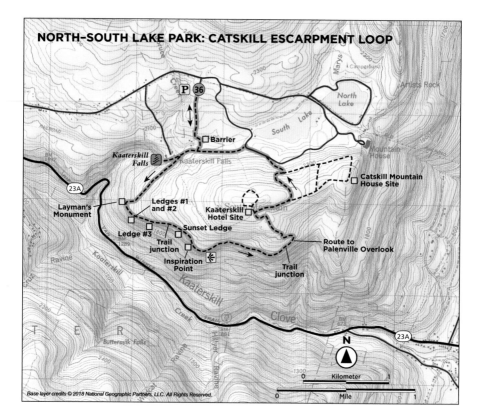

NORTH–SOUTH LAKE PARK: CATSKILL ESCARPMENT LOOP

Base layer credits © 2018 National Geographic Partners, LLC. All Rights Reserved.

0.6 Stop and register at the registry box. In a few minutes you will reach a major trail junction; go right on the Escarpment Trail (blue markers). If you want to explore a side trail right away, follow the signs across a bridge to your right. This takes you to a viewpoint for the top portion of magnificent Kaaterskill Falls, one of the tallest and most photographed falls in New York State. This side trail adds only about 0.4 mile to your overall hike.

1.2 Reach Layman's Monument. The trail turns left (east) here; continue to follow it. This part of the trail can be very wet in spring and early summer, or after a hard rain.

1.3 Just after a scramble up some large rocks, reach the first of several ledges (overlooks). This one provides a great view of Santa Cruz Falls and Buttermilk Ravine, where you may glimpse Buttermilk Falls.

1.4 This overlook provides more views of Buttermilk Falls and Buttermilk Ravine.

1.6 The yellow- and blue-blazed trails cross here. Continue straight on the Escarpment (blue-blazed) trail. (The yellow-blazed trail goes back to Scutt Road.)

1.7 At Sunset Ledge, you can look west toward Haines Falls and enjoy an iconic view of the Catskills.

1.8   Inspiration Point offers an exceptional view of the edge of the Catskills and the valley beyond.

2.0   This overlook furnishes views of Poet's Ledge, Viola Ravine and Falls, Wildcat Ravine, Indian Head Ledge, and Buttermilk Ravine. The peaks in front of you are Kaaterskill High Peak and Round Top Mountain.

2.6   At the trail junction turn right on the Escarpment Trail. (The other trail will take you back to the parking area.) In less than 0.5 mile, another trail junction offers a route to Palenville Overlook and Palenville; bear left to stay on the Escarpment Trail loop.

3.0   At the junction with the trail to the Kaaterskill Hotel site, go straight for the short loop around the former hotel site or turn right on the Escarpment Trail.

3.3   Come to the junction with the trail to North-South Lake. Turn left to go to the lake, or keep going straight to visit Boulder Rock and the Catskill Mountain House site. This adds about 1.0 mile to your total hike but features some terrific views. When you're ready, continue left on this trail to North-South Lake. Watch your step on the Horseshoe Corner.

3.8   Reach North Lake Road and turn left on the road.

3.9   At the cross-country ski trail, turn left (off the road). Rejoin the main trail.

4.3   You're back at the beginning of the main trail. Turn right to return to your vehicle.

4.9   Arrive back at the parking area.

37. KAATERSKILL AND BASTION FALLS

WHY GO?

The tallest waterfall in New York State is one of the Catskills' most visited natural areas.

THE RUNDOWN

Start: Kaaterskill Clove parking area on NY 23A
Elevation gain: 98 feet
Distance: 1.2 miles out and back
Difficulty: Strenuous
Hiking time: About 1.25 hours
Seasons: Spring and summer, and after a heavy rain
Schedule: Trail open daily, dawn to dusk
Fees and permits: No fees or permits required
Trail contact: NYSDEC Division of Lands & Forests, 625 Broadway, Fifth Floor, Albany, NY 12233; (518) 473-9518; dec.ny.gov/lands/80993.html
Dog-friendly: Dogs permitted on leash
Trail surface: Dirt path and rock steps/ledges

Land status: New York State Department of Environmental Conservation (NYSDEC)
Nearest towns: Catskill and Hunter, New York
Other trail users: Hikers only
Maps: NatGeo TOPO! Map (USGS): Kaaterskill Clove; NatGeo Trails Illustrated Map #755: Catskill Park; trail map available at catskillmountaineer.com/NSL-KF .html
Special considerations: This trail can be dangerous in wet or icy conditions. Many people have been killed when they walked out in front of the top drop. Others have been killed by falling from the top of the falls. Stay on the trail.

FINDING THE TRAILHEAD

From the town of Catskill, take NY 23A West for 13.2 miles to the bend in the road at Bastion Falls. Pass the falls and turn into the parking area on the left side of the road, about 0.2 mile after the falls.
Trailhead GPS: N42 11.387' / W74 04.456'

WHAT TO SEE

If you only have time to take one hike in the Catskill Mountains, make it this one—a challenging 0.5 mile up a narrow, rocky path to one of the finest sights in the entire park. Kaaterskill Falls is taller than any of Niagara's three falls, and its towering geological setting provides the payoff for the half-hour of scrambling you will do to get up here.

The trail to Bastion and Kaaterskill Falls leads along the highway, so keep your wits about you.

Do the falls look familiar, even though you've never been here? Perhaps you're a fan of the Hudson River School of American artists, many of whom painted iconic landscapes featuring Kaaterskill Falls. As far back as 1825, artist Thomas Cole discovered the charms of this wilderness after reading about it in Washington Irving's famous short story "Rip Van Winkle." His remarkable painting of the falls became a cover of the *New York Evening Post*, attracting many other artists to settle in nearby Palenville and paint Kaaterskill Falls and other gorgeous sights in the Catskill region. These paintings became the impetus for tourists to travel here to see the falls and the Catskill Mountains for themselves, launching more than a century and a half of intensive tourist activity in this remote part of New York State.

This waterfall, like so many in New York, splits into two distinct sections. The first is a stunning sheer drop from a notch at the top of the gorge, pouring down to a hanging valley. The flow's force pushes on to a second drop, this one a segmented cascade that falls into a boulder-laden pool directly below. From here Spruce Creek continues down the mountain as whitecaps, frills, and the occasional rapid. Plenty of large glacial errata provide places where you can sit or stand directly in front of the falls and admire the entire phenomenon. The most energetic visitors climb to the falls' second level and walk out in front of the water's sheer drop. We don't recommend this, especially in high water months, but you will see people doing it.

Pass Bastion Falls on your way to the Kaaterskill Falls trail.

On your way to Kaaterskill, you'll spot Bastion Falls right on NY 23A, and I want to give this entirely likable falls its due. It flows at the entrance to the Kaaterskill Falls trail, providing a sort of aquatic appetizer to the main course farther up. For those who feel that the hike to Kaaterskill may be too strenuous, it's possible to feel satisfied with this impressive cascade that's viewable from the roadside. Be careful if you pull off and get out of your car here; this bend in the road can be a blind corner for cars coming around it from the south.

This hike gets crowded in May and June, even in the middle of the week. We encountered busloads of college students, day campers, retirees, young vacationing couples, families with children, tourists from European countries, an artist and her Jack Russell terrier, and even a trail maintenance crew from the Adirondack Mountain Club—and we were there on a Thursday. Come early in the day or late in the afternoon to get a parking space.

MILES AND DIRECTIONS

0.0 Start at the parking area, cross the road, and step over the guardrail to be out of the line of traffic. The road's construction will force you back onto the shoulder for short distances, so stay over to the side as far as you can.

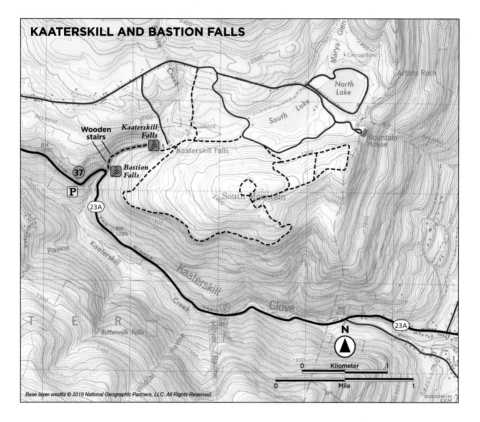

KAATERSKILL AND BASTION FALLS

0.3 Arrive at Bastion Falls. The trail to Kaaterskill Falls begins just past Bastion; you'll see a clearly marked trailhead. Begin the ascent. Climb a long series of staircase-like boulders to a wooden staircase. After the stairs, the trail levels off for a bit.

0.4 Climb another wooden staircase. From here the trail follows closely along the creek but is fairly level for a while. Cross several small streams on rocks.

0.6 A last scramble and rock-hop take you to a clear view of the magnificent falls from the bottom. There are plenty of large slabs of rock and big boulders here if you want to sit and contemplate the double cascade. When you're ready, head back down the way you came. Watch out for wet, slippery rocks as you descend.

0.9 You're back at Bastion Falls. Take a last look before you head back down the road to the parking area.

1.2 Arrive back at the parking area.

WESTERN CONNECTICUT

Just over the state border and at the eastern edge of the Taconic Mountains, another river creates a valley of its own, one named by the Mohicans for its position "beyond the mountain." The Housatonic River provided Native Americans with summer passage southward from its source in the Berkshire Mountains of Massachusetts, joining the Naugatuck River in present-day Shelton before reaching its end at Long Island Sound. It is said that hiking trails through the region follow the routes the Mohicans and Algonquins used to travel south to fish and north to trap animals and gather furs for trading.

Here the ridges of ancient mountains form a major fault system in which weather, wind, and time have worn away the younger rock to expose the older bedrock "overthrust" beneath—while maintaining a much newer layer beneath it. This neat geological trick makes the Housatonic Range an exciting place to explore for its unusual rock

Steep Rock Preserve is a highlight of any trip to Western Connecticut.

formations, its steep but mercifully brief climbs, and its mountaintop views across an expansive valley of farmlands, orchards, and inviting New England villages.

Whether you have already discovered the Housatonic Valley or have yet to venture this far east, these three hikes will open your eyes to new scenic and natural wonders in the peaceful Connecticut high country. If you're looking for an outdoor experience closer to the state's southern coast, take the Metro-North Railroad to Greenwich and explore a carefully preserved wetland and woods, one of the many places in this region that enlightened landowners took steps to keep forever wild.

38. THE AUDUBON CENTER IN GREENWICH

WHY GO?
An orchard, woods, a lake, and miles of well-groomed trails—this is an oasis of natural tranquility.

THE RUNDOWN

Start: Parking area at the Kimberlin Nature Education Center
Elevation gain: 224 feet
Distance: 2.6-mile lollipop
Difficulty: Easy
Hiking time: About 1.5 hours
Seasons: Year-round
Schedule: Trails open daily, sunrise to sunset
Fees and permits: Admission charge per adult, reduced for children and seniors, and free to Audubon members
Trail contact: The Audubon Center in Greenwich, 613 Riverside Rd., Greenwich, CT 06831; (203) 869-5272; greenwich.audubon.org

Dog-friendly: Dogs not permitted
Trail surface: Mowed grass, woodland floor, boardwalks
Land status: Audubon Center
Nearest town: Greenwich, Connecticut
Other trail users: Joggers
Maps: NatGeo TOPO! Map (USGS): Glenville, CT; trail map available online at greenwich.audubon.org/sites/g/files/amh711/f/greenwich_trail_map.pdf
Special considerations: Trail access may be limited from early fall through midwinter due to land management activities.

FINDING THE TRAILHEAD

From I-684 or Route 22 in New York, take I-684 to exit 3 (Armonk) and turn north onto NY 22. At the traffic light, turn right onto North Greenwich Road. Continue 2 miles to John Street. The entrance is on the left.

From I-95 in Connecticut, take I-95 to exit 3 and turn north onto Arch Street. Immediately after the light at Railroad Avenue, turn left onto Sound View Drive. At the end of Sound View, turn right onto Field Point Road. Turn left onto Brookside Drive and continue to the end of the street; turn left onto Glenville Road. Drive 1.5 miles to Riversville Road; turn right. Continue 4.5 miles to John Street. The entrance gate is on your right.

Trailhead GPS: N41 05.790' / W73 41.291'

WHAT TO SEE
If ever there was a place that gave testimony to the value of preserving open space for wild critters and human beings alike, this 285-acre Audubon sanctuary in the heart of densely populated Greenwich is it. The whisper of millions of leaves in gentle winds,

A central pond is a highlight at the Greenwich Audubon Center.

The former homestead buildings have become the Kimberlin Nature Education Center.

Boardwalks help keep your feet dry as you walk through the woods.

WHAT'S A VERNAL POOL?

Small, seasonal ponds that fill with water in spring but dry up in summer are known as vernal (or ephemeral) pools. They provide temporary homes for small amphibians like frogs and salamanders. Because they come and go fairly quickly, these pools don't host fish species, making them the perfect places for tiny creatures to gain a foothold in the world—literally in this case—before they reach maturity and move on to live in the surrounding forest. Keep an eye out for tiny hopping or slithering creatures as you walk the trails in spring and early summer, especially if it's been a particularly wet season.

the rustlings of chipmunks and squirrels making their way through the lush understory, the whistles and chirrups of tiny warblers and vireos among the trees, and the giggles of children discovering their first frog or turtle all generate an immediate sense of gratitude that such a place can still exist.

There's no doubt that migrating birds find this place especially useful. The Audubon Center in Greenwich holds a strategic position on the Atlantic Flyway, the route that millions—some say billions—of birds take annually on their way to their summer breeding grounds here and farther north, and again in fall as they travel south to warmer climates in Central and South America. Whether they use this sanctuary as a stopover or stay the season, these birds could not survive the challenging journey without the plentiful sources of natural foods they find here, as well as the shelter from predators they enjoy under the concealing canopy. Baltimore oriole, blue-winged warbler, and Louisiana waterthrush find season-long protection here, as do ovenbird, scarlet tanager, and wood thrush.

Birds thrive here for another reason: the unbroken period of protection they have found at the Audubon Center in Greenwich for many decades. Landowners Eleanor Clovis Reese and H. Hall Clovis donated this land to Audubon all the way back in 1942, making this the National Audubon Society's first educational center in the United States. The original New England homestead buildings have been joined by the Kimberlin Nature Education Center, where your adventure can begin in the visitor center. Pick up a map of the entire preserve and its 7 miles of trails so you can decide if you'd like to explore one of the many trails that diverge from the Lake Trail loop we have described below.

You have the option of traversing hardwood forests of maple, beech, and oak; open meadows filled with wildflowers in spring and summer; the circumference of man-made Mead Lake with its blinds for birding, especially during the waterfowl migrations in spring and fall; and red maple swamps that provide homes to veery and waterthrush. Watch and listen for rustlings that may reveal a river otter, muskrat, white-tailed deer, wild turkey, or flying squirrel—even a coyote or a bat if you're walking toward sunset. In the fall you might glimpse a saw-whet owl at rest in a dense shrub. Stop back at the visitor center at the end of your hike to record your bird and animal observations in the Wildlife Sightings Log.

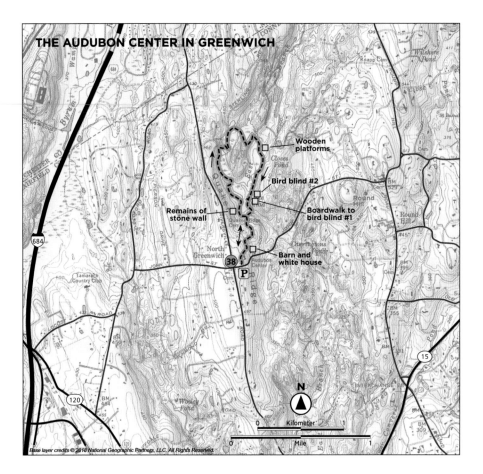

THE AUDUBON CENTER IN GREENWICH

Wooden platforms

Bird blind #2

Remains of stone wall

Boardwalk to bird blind #1

North Greenwich

38

P

Barn and white house

N

MILES AND DIRECTIONS

0.0 Start from the visitor center, take the paved lane (service road), and turn left onto the Lake Trail. Pass the barns and the white house, and turn left onto the mowed grass path east of the white house. The meadow is on your right. Note the beehives on your left as you approach the apple orchard.

0.2 Turn right to walk into the orchard. Continue straight past the grass paths toward the woods.

0.3 At the intersection, go straight across on the Lake Trail. This is a crushed-cinder path. At the next intersection, bear left on the Lake Trail. Descend for a while into a beech and maple forest.

0.4 The Lake Trail loop begins. Turn left. Sections of boardwalk alternate with the trail to the lake.

0.5 Pass a stone wall as the lake comes into view. The boardwalk comes up on your right; continue straight (you'll do the boardwalk later).

0.8 Cross a stream on rocks. At the next intersection go left on the Beech Hill Trail. Then bear left at the next intersection onto the Dogwood Trail. Cross a stream on a boardwalk.

0.9 At this intersection, go right on the Dogwood Trail.

1.1 At the Dogwood Lane sign, turn right. At the top of the hill, turn left on the Maple Swamp loop. Follow the top of the ridge.

1.3 Turn left on the Hemlock Trail. This section may be mucky after a rain.

1.6 Turn right onto Riverbottom Road.

1.7 A short boardwalk goes over a stream.

1.8 The Old Pasture Trail goes left. Continue straight.

1.9 The Lake Trail goes right. Continue straight.

2.0 The Riverbottom and Lake Trails split. Bear right on the Lake Trail for great lake views. A bird blind comes up on your right.

2.1 Take the boardwalk to another bird blind. When you're ready, continue on the Lake Trail.

2.2 Cross some large rocks to reach the bridge over the lake's spillway.

2.3 Follow the signs back to the nature center to return to your vehicle.

2.6 Arrive back at the parking area.

39. LION'S HEAD

📷

WHY GO?

A short uphill climb brings you to one of the most magnificent views in Connecticut.

THE RUNDOWN

Start: Parking area at the end of Bunker Hill Road in Salisbury
Elevation gain: 591 feet
Distance: 4.0 miles out and back
Difficulty: Strenuous
Hiking time: About 2 hours
Seasons: Spring through fall
Schedule: Open daily, dawn to dusk
Fees and permits: No fees or permits required
Trail contact: Salisbury Parks and Forest Commission, Town of Salisbury, 27 Main St., Salisbury, CT 06068; (860) 435-0287; salisburyct.us
Dog-friendly: Dogs permitted on leash

Trail surface: Dirt and rock
Land status: Edith Scoville Memorial Sanctuary
Nearest town: Salisbury, Connecticut
Other trail users: Hikers only
Maps: NatGeo TOPO! Map (USGS): Sharon, CT; NatGeo Trails Illustrated Map #1509: Appalachian Trail, Schaghticoke Mountain to East Mountain; trail map available online at berkshirehiking.com/hikes/lionshead.html
Special considerations: This is a steep trail and is not recommended for people with heart or lung issues.

FINDING THE TRAILHEAD

From I-84 in Connecticut, take exit 7 and head north on US 202/ US 7. Stay on US 7 about 32 miles then bear left on CT 112. In 6 miles turn right on US 44 and continue into the town of Salisbury. At the junction with CT 41 (Under Mountain Road), bear left onto CT 41. Continue to the Appalachian Trail parking area on the left side of the road.
Trailhead GPS: N41 59.730' / W73 25.689'

WHAT TO SEE

If you're looking for a quick hike to an incredible view and you're not afraid to take on some challenge, Lion's Head fits the bill. Just a small peak along a mountain ridge in the Housatonic Range, Lion's Head is part of the overthrust of ancient rock that somehow dominates the younger rock below it, a geological sleight of hand caused by eons of erosion. The result provides a welcome reward for hikers who brave the steep trail to the top—the kind of view that makes you stop and say, "Yes, this is why I love hiking."

It's worth the struggle to reach this summit at 1,738 feet.

LIONS HEAD
ELEV 1738

What will you see? The entire Housatonic River Valley spreads before you, with the sweet town of Salisbury to the east and the Litchfield Hills to the south, with Bear Mountain (not the New York one, but the highest peak in Connecticut, at 2,316 feet) dominating the landscape, as well as Mount Everett and Mount Race just beyond Bear. On a crystal-clear day, you can see Mount Greylock, the highest peak in Massachusetts, some 45 miles north. The two lakes you see directly to the east are known, aptly, as Twin Lakes. In between, farmlands let you know that the northeast region's food supply is healthy and thriving, while villages and hamlets appear between the folds of the foothills.

The Appalachian Trail provides the route to the top of Lion's Head, providing a taste of the 51 miles of white-blazed trail that traverses Connecticut on its way north and south. You have the option of taking the AT all the way up to the summit—a route that goes nearly straight up as you approach the top, giving you the chance to do some serious scrambling up an exposed rock face. Or you can take the trail junction just before you reach the rock face and follow the more gradual Lion's Head trail, especially as this section comes during the last gasp before you reach the top. You'll see AT hikers with heavily loaded packs opting for the easier route.

See the expanse of western Connecticut from the top of Lion's Head.

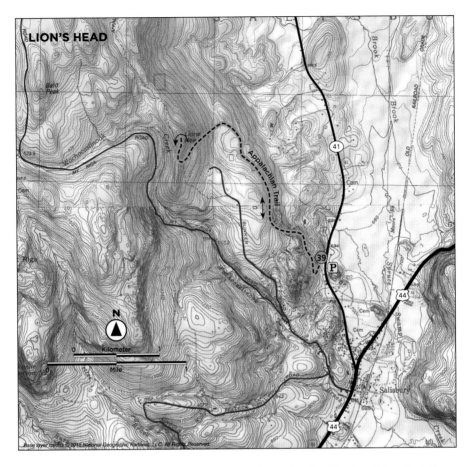

From here the AT continues up Bear Mountain before heading into New York State, descending from Lion's Head to a ridge just below the peak and moving on to the trail's Riga shelter, where hikers can camp before the ascent of Bear.

MILES AND DIRECTIONS

0.0 Start at the trailhead in the northwest corner of the parking area. Follow the white AT blazes.

0.8 The blue blazes of the local trail join you here. Continue following the AT's white blazes.

1.0 The trail levels off; then the blue blazes split off. The AT goes straight up a rock face for a challenging scramble. The Lion's Head trail (blue) goes straight and meanders around the big rocks. It's your choice of which to follow; we took the blue trail.

THIS IS A TURKEY VULTURE

It happens all the time: We reach a summit and see large black birds with red heads circling at nearly eye level or below us, and a hiker from another party cries out, "Look at the eagle!"

Generally, it's not an eagle. The feather-less red head and the all-black body are giveaways—what birders call "diagnos-tic"—when it comes to soaring birds. These are turkey vultures, and they often soar in groups of three or more near the tops of New York's smaller peaks. You also can recognize them by the slight V their wings make in relation to their bodies, a position called a dihedral.

Turkey vultures are one of the largest birds in the United States, so they are often mistaken for eagles. These carrion-eaters have no interest in you; they're looking for recent roadkill or morsels left behind by meat-eating animals. They soar for long periods (usually with barely a flap of their wings) and cover great distances, and while they may land on a ledge near you to keep watch for their next meal, they pose no threat to you or your lunch.

Eagles are close in size to turkey vultures, but they have an entirely different head shape, and the adult eagles have the characteristic white head, yellow bill, and white tail. Young eagles may appear uniformly brown, but you will see some white mottling on their heads and bodies up close—and their heads are entirely covered in feathers.

1.1 This last 0.1 mile is a steep climb up rock steps and then a level stretch and one last (not as steep) climb. The AT goes left and right. Turn right, and con-tinue up.

2.0 Reach the summit, where you are rewarded with a tremendous view. When you are ready, return the way you came.

4.0 Arrive back at the parking area.

40. STEEP ROCK PRESERVE: STEEP ROCK LOOP

📷

WHY GO?

A summit to a sumptuous view, a suspension bridge, a deep forest, and a burbling river make this a must-do trail.

THE RUNDOWN

Start: Parking area at the junction of Lower Church Hill and River Roads at the northern end of the preserve
Elevation gain: 410 feet
Distance: 4.0-mile loop
Difficulty: Moderate
Hiking time: 2 hours
Seasons: Spring through fall
Schedule: Open daily, sunrise to sunset
Fees and permits: No fees or permits required; donations welcome
Trail contact: Steep Rock Association, Inc., PO Box 279, Washington Depot, CT 06794; (860) 868-9131; steeprockassoc.org
Dog-friendly: Dogs permitted on leash

Trail surface: Dirt and rock
Land status: Steep Rock Association land trust
Nearest town: Washington Depot, Connecticut
Other trail users: Mountain bikers and equestrians on eastern portion of the yellow-blazed trail; equestrians on parts of the west portion of the yellow-blazed trail
Maps: NatGeo TOPO! Map (USGS): New Preston, CT; trail map available online at steeprockassoc.org/dir/wp-content/uploads/2013/05/map_steep_rock.pdf
Special considerations: Tunnel Road south of Spring Hill Road is closed in winter.

FINDING THE TRAILHEAD

From I-84, take US 7 North 41 miles to Still River Drive in New Milford. Turn right onto Still River Drive, and continue as it becomes Grove Street. In 2.3 miles turn right onto NY 109 (Chestnut Land Road). Continue 6 miles to Fenn Hill Road; turn right. Turn left onto West Church Hill Road, and continue onto Lower Church Hill Road. In about 0.5 mile, the preserve parking area is on your left.
Trailhead GPS: N41 37.318' / W73 19.566'

WHAT TO SEE

Imagine that you are about to build your dream house, but just as the steam shovels prepare to break ground, you get word that a timber company intends to strip all the trees from the hillsides you will view from your windows. What do you do? That's the dilemma faced by architect Ehrick Rossiter in 1889, and it impelled him to make a bold

On a crisp fall day or in midsummer, a hike to Steep Rock is a delight.

From Steep Rock, the view of western Connecticut is unsurpassed.

move—one that had an impact we still feel today. Rossiter took the money for his dream country home and used it to buy the land from the timber company. He didn't build his house until some years later, but he saved 100 acres of pristine forest, building carriage roads and bridges over the Shepaug River and opening the land to his friends and to the residents of Washington, Connecticut.

When it came time for Rossiter to decide the fate of the land beyond his own lifetime, he put together a board of trustees to whom he entrusted the care of his property in perpetuity. Four years later, the trustees purchased the area known as the Clam Shell, including the summit of Steep Rock, forever protecting this viewpoint for generations of hikers to come. Not only did Rossiter set an example that other landowners would eventually follow, but he essentially launched a movement in Litchfield County, one that has resulted in the preservation of more than 2,700 acres of land by the organization he helped to found.

Today you can enjoy the 974-acre Steep Rock Preserve on this loop trail, which leads to a splendid viewpoint at the Steep Rock summit—a fairly challenging climb to the top at an elevation of 776 feet, but not nearly as difficult as Lion's Head or any of the Hudson Highlands summits. From here you can enjoy a classic view of the original 100 heavily forested acres that Rossiter chose to preserve and for miles beyond, a survey of the Washington area with the region's iconic emerald hills and fertile valleys.

If you live in the area and find yourself captivated by Steep Rock Preserve, you may want to deepen your relationship with it by participating in a citizen science project. Volunteers count bald eagles on the Shepaug River in the middle of winter, a wonderful

You'll find plenty of places to pause and admire the scenery.

reason to get outside and into a natural area at a time you might normally cocoon yourself indoors. Some learn to recognize and differentiate the calls of a variety of frogs and spend evenings listening for them in this and other wetlands owned by the Steep Rock Association. Others monitor the nest boxes within the preserves, checking to see what species are using the boxes, how many nestlings they have, and whether brown-headed cowbirds have added their own eggs to the nests of these birds. There's plenty to do if you'd like a great excuse to spend more time in the wilds of Connecticut—and the knowledge you gain will increase your enjoyment of trails throughout the region.

MILES AND DIRECTIONS

0.0   Start from the parking area and take the trail with yellow markers.

0.6   At the intersection, go right on the yellow trail. In a moment, another trail goes left; continue straight.

0.9   Turn right to head to the summit. In a moment the white trail goes straight and yellow-blazed trail turns left. Go left.

1.1   The yellow trail goes left and right. Go right to the summit.

1.3   Reach the summit. When you're ready, go back down the trail and bear right at the fork, continuing on the yellow trail to loop around the Shepaug River.

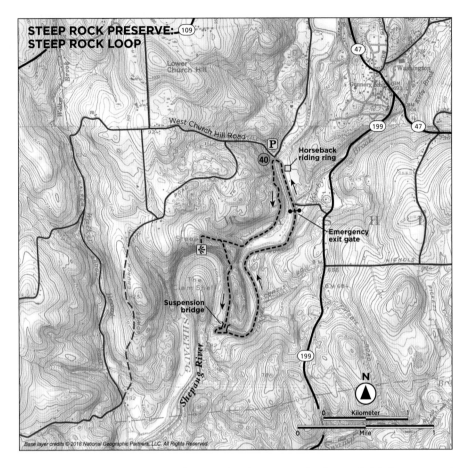

1.7 A yellow arrow points right; go right. The green and yellow trails join here.

1.8 The green trail goes right. Continue straight on the yellow trail.

2.1 The white trail goes right. Continue straight.

2.3 A suspension bridge crosses the Shepaug River. Cross the bridge and turn right on the yellow trail.

3.6 Come to an emergency exit gate; then a parking area and a road goes right and left. Continue left onto Tunnel Road.

3.8 Continue straight on the yellow trail, which runs along Tunnel Road (open for vehicles spring through fall). (**Option:** For an alternative, non-vehicular route, cross to the blue trail, which parallels the yellow trail along Tunnel Road for about 0.75 mile until it meets back up again with the yellow trail.)

4.0 There's a riding ring to the right. In a moment, arrive back at the parking area.

BONUS HIKES

Literally thousands of miles of trails crisscross the Hudson River Valley, some of which are extremely popular with hikers coming up from New York City or down from the Capital Region. So far in this book, I've provided detailed information about some of the most famous, the most notorious, and some lesser-known trails that I'm sure you will enjoy. As I noted in the introduction, this book is like a tasting menu—a sampling of some of the Hudson Valley's most spectacular and fascinating places—so that you can decide where you'd like to explore further.

I want to be sure you can find your way to the popular trails in well-known places like Harriman State Park, Mohonk Preserve (which I have not mentioned before because of the high fees for hiking there), Shawangunk Ridge, and the Hudson Highlands, as well as some of the most pleasant easy hikes throughout the valley. The brief descriptions, directions, and special considerations provided here will help you choose your next adventure.

OLANA STATE HISTORIC SITE

Start: Park in the lot at the top of the property, nearest the house, and take the brick stairway to the carriage road.
Elevation gain: 162 feet
Distance: 1.2-mile loop
Difficulty: Easy
Hiking time: About 45 minutes
Seasons: Spring through fall
Schedule: Trails open daily, 8 a.m. to sunset
Fees and permits: Fee for grounds access on weekends and holidays, Apr through Oct. To avoid the fee, park in the lot at the bottom of the hill and walk up.

Trail contact: Olana State Historic Site, 5720 SR 9G, Hudson, NY 12534; (518) 828-0135; olana.org
Dog-friendly: Dogs permitted on leash
Trail surface: Crushed shale and paved paths
Land status: New York state historic site
Nearest town: Hudson, New York
Other trail users: Joggers; cross-country skiers in season
Special considerations: The admission fee can be credited toward a tour of the house. Reservations are recommended for house tours.

POET'S WALK PARK

Start: Parking area at the Poet's Walk Park entrance, off CR 103 (River Road) in Red Hook
Elevation gain: 249 feet
Distance: 2.2-mile lollipop
Difficulty: Easy
Hiking time: About 1.25 hours
Seasons: Spring through fall
Schedule: Open daily, 9 a.m. to seasonal closing time (generally sunset)
Fees and permits: No fees or permits required
Trail contact: Scenic Hudson, One Civic Center Plaza, Suite 200, Poughkeepsie, NY 12601; (845) 473-4440; scenichudson.org
Dog-friendly: Dogs permitted on leash
Trail surface: Mowed and gravel paths
Land status: Scenic Hudson property
Nearest town: Red Hook, New York
Other trail users: Trail runners; birders; cross-country skiers in season
Special considerations: People really do come here to read or write poetry. Please respect their desire for quiet contemplation.

PAWLING NATURE RESERVE

Start: Parking area on Quaker Lake Road, off CR 68 (North Quaker Hill Road) in Pawling
Elevation gain: 1,079 feet
Distance: 7.7-mile loop
Difficulty: Moderate
Hiking time: About 4 hours
Seasons: Spring through fall
Schedule: Open daily, sunrise to sunset
Fees and permits: No fees or permits required
Trail contact: The Nature Conservancy, 195 New Karner Rd., Suite 200, Albany, NY 12205; (518) 690-7850; nature.org
Dog-friendly: Dogs not permitted
Trail surface: Dirt path
Land status: The Nature Conservancy property
Nearest town: Pawling, New York
Other trail users: Appalachian Trail thru-hikers and section hikers
Special considerations: Deer hunting is permitted here in season (usually Nov and Dec). Wear orange if you hike during hunting season, or consider planning your hike for another time.

HUNTER BROOK PRESERVE

Start: Parking area on Fox Tail Lane in Yorktown, off Hunter Brook Road
Elevation gain: 358 feet
Distance: 2.5-mile lollipop
Difficulty: Easy
Hiking time: About 1.5 hours
Seasons: Spring through fall
Schedule: Open daily, dawn to dusk
Fees and permits: No fees or permits required
Trail contact: Westchester Land Trust, 403 Harris Rd., Bedford Hills, NY 10507; (914) 241-6346; westchesterlandtrust.org
Dog-friendly: Dogs permitted on leash
Trail surface: Dirt path
Land status: Westchester Land Trust
Nearest town: Yorktown, New York
Other trail users: Hikers only
Special considerations: Watch for poison ivy and ticks.

MIANUS RIVER GORGE PRESERVE

Start: Preserve parking area off Mianus River Road in Bedford
Elevation gain: 620 feet
Distance: 4.2-mile loop
Difficulty: Easy
Hiking time: About 2.5 hours
Seasons: Spring through fall
Schedule: Open daily, Apr 1–Nov 30, 8:30 a.m. to 5 p.m.; closed Dec 1–Mar 31
Fees and permits: No fees or permits required
Trail contact: Mianus River Gorge Preserve, Inc., 167 Mianus River Rd., Bedford, NY 10506; (914) 234-3455; www. mianus.org
Dog-friendly: Dogs not permitted
Trail surface: Dirt path
Land status: Owned and managed by Mianus River Gorge Inc.
Nearest town: Bedford, New York
Other trail users: Hikers only
Special considerations: The preserve is closed in winter. Insect repellent is highly recommended here in any open season.

HARRIMAN STATE PARK: POPOLOPEN TORNE

Start: In the Fort Montgomery parking area on US 9W, just before Highland Falls
Elevation gain: 1,381 feet
Distance: 5.1-mile loop
Difficulty: Strenuous
Hiking time: About 3 hours
Seasons: Spring through fall
Schedule: Open daily, dawn to dusk
Fees and permits: No fees or permits required
Trail contact: Palisades Interstate Park Commission, Bear Mountain, NY 10911; (845) 786-2701; nysparks.state.ny.us/parks/145/details.aspx
Dog-friendly: Dogs permitted on leash
Trail surface: Dirt and rocks
Land status: New York state park
Nearest town: Highland Falls, New York
Other trail users: Hikers only
Special considerations: Boots with ankle support are a must for this park. This trail runs parallel to the Palisades Interstate Parkway and along a suburban neighborhood, so road noise is part of the experience.

HARRIMAN STATE PARK: TIMP-TORNE TRAIL

Start: Parking area at Anthony Wayne Recreation Area, off the Palisades Parkway
Elevation gain: 1,217 feet
Distance: 7.1-mile lollipop
Difficulty: Strenuous
Hiking time: About 4 hours
Seasons: Spring through fall
Schedule: Open daily, dawn to dusk
Fees and permits: No fees or permits required
Trail contact: Palisades Interstate Park Commission, Bear Mountain, NY 10911; (845) 786-2701; nysparks.state .ny.us/parks/145/details.aspx

Dog-friendly: Dogs permitted on leash
Trail surface: Dirt and rocks
Land status: New York state park
Nearest town: Highland Falls, New York
Other trail users: Trail runners; cross-country skiers on some sections in season
Special considerations: Insect repellent is a must on this trail. Long pants are recommended, as there are brushy sections. Watch carefully for trail markers; some parts of the trail can be confusing because of all the intersections.

HARRIMAN STATE PARK: RAMAPO-DUNDERBERG TRAIL

Start: Parking area off Tuxedo Road in Harriman State Park
Elevation gain: 1,392 feet
Distance: 21.7-mile backpacking shuttle
Difficulty: Strenuous
Hiking time: About 3 days
Seasons: Spring through fall
Schedule: Open daily, dawn to dusk
Fees and permits: No fees or permits required
Trail contact: Palisades Interstate Park Commission, Bear Mountain, NY 10911; (845) 786-2701; nysparks.state .ny.us/parks/145/details.aspx

Dog-friendly: Dogs permitted on leash
Trail surface: Dirt, rocks, large open rock faces
Land status: New York state park
Nearest town: Tuxedo Park, New York, at the western end; Peekskill, New York, at the eastern end
Other trail users: Trail runners; mountain bikers in some sections
Special considerations: This trail involves steep climbs and some scrambling.

BEAR MOUNTAIN STATE PARK: DOODLETOWN BRIDLE PATH LOOP

Start: Parking area north of Iona Island Road on US 9W/ 202
Elevation gain: 1,252 feet
Distance: 5.7-mile loop
Difficulty: Moderate
Hiking time: About 3 hours
Seasons: Spring through fall
Schedule: Open daily, dawn to dusk
Fees and permits: No fees or permits required
Trail contact: Palisades Interstate Park Commission, Bear Mountain, NY 10911; (845) 786-2701; nysparks.state .ny.us/parks/145/details.aspx

Dog-friendly: Dogs permitted on leash
Trail surface: Some crumbling pavement, some rocky dirt path, large sections of a wide bridle path
Land status: New York state park
Nearest town: Fort Montgomery, New York
Other trail users: Equestrians, trail runners, joggers, mountain bikers
Special considerations: Many trails crisscross this one. The New York–New Jersey Trail Conference map of this area is a must for making certain you are on the right trail.

BEAR MOUNTAIN STATE PARK: MAJOR WELCH TRAIL

Start: Parking area off Seven Lakes Drive, east of the Bear Mountain Inn and Overlook Lodge
Elevation gain: 1,128 feet
Distance: 4.0-mile loop
Difficulty: Strenuous
Hiking time: About 3 hours
Seasons: Spring through fall
Schedule: Open daily, dawn to dusk
Fees and permits: No fees or permits required
Trail contact: Palisades Interstate Park Commission, Bear Mountain, NY 10911; (845) 786-2701; nysparks.state .ny.us/parks/13/details.aspx

Dog-friendly: Dogs permitted on leash
Trail surface: Dirt and rocks
Land status: New York state park
Nearest town: Tompkins Cove, New York
Other trail users: Trail runners
Special considerations: The Jolly Rovers volunteer trail crew of the New York–New Jersey Trail Conference, with the help of AmeriCorps interns and professional trail builders, recently reconstructed a large section of this trail. New stone steps make the trail easier to navigate and safer for hikers.

HUDSON HIGHLANDS STATE PARK PRESERVE: WASHBURN TRAIL TO TAURUS MOUNTAIN

Start: Little Stony Point trailhead off NY 9D in Hudson Highlands State Park
Elevation gain: 1,319 feet
Distance: 4.8 miles out and back
Difficulty: Strenuous
Hiking time: About 3 hours
Seasons: Spring through fall
Schedule: Open daily, dawn to dusk
Fees and permits: No fees or permits required
Trail contact: Hudson Highlands State Park Preserve, Route 9D, Beacon, NY 10512; (845) 225-7207; parks.ny.gov/parks/9/hunting.aspx

Dog-friendly: Dogs permitted on leash
Trail surface: Dirt path with some very rocky sections
Land status: New York state park preserve
Nearest town: Cold Spring, New York
Other trail users: Trail runners
Special considerations: Boots with ankle support and a walking stick or poles are must-haves for this challenging hike through areas strewn with many boulders.

HUDSON HIGHLANDS STATE PARK PRESERVE: WILKINSON MEMORIAL TRAIL TO SUGARLOAF MOUNTAIN

Start: Parking area on Breakneck Road (NY 9D) or Metro-North stop for Breakneck Ridge–Northbound
Elevation gain: 843 feet
Distance: 2.9-mile lollipop
Difficulty: Moderate
Hiking time: About 1.5 hours
Seasons: Spring through fall
Schedule: Open daily, dawn to dusk
Fees and permits: No fees or permits required
Trail contact: Hudson Highlands State Park Preserve, Route 9D, Beacon, NY 10512; (845) 225-7207; parks.ny.gov/parks/9/hunting.aspx
Dog-friendly: Dogs permitted on leash

Trail surface: Dirt path with some rocky sections
Land status: New York state park preserve
Nearest town: Cold Spring, New York
Other trail users: Trail runners
Special considerations: This trail can be very crowded on weekends, as people come up from New York City via Metro-North to go hiking. Consider hiking on a weekday.

BEACON MEMORIAL PARK: FISHKILL RIDGE

Start: Parking area at the end of Mountain Brook Drive in Beacon
Elevation gain: 1,092 feet
Distance: 6.4 miles out and back
Difficulty: Moderate
Hiking time: About 4 hours
Seasons: Spring through fall
Schedule: Open daily, dawn to dusk
Fees and permits: No fees or permits required
Trail contact: City of Beacon, 1 Municipal Plaza, Beacon, NY 12508; (845) 838-5000; cityofbeacon.org

Dog-friendly: Dogs permitted on leash
Trail surface: Dirt path
Land status: City park
Nearest town: Beacon, New York
Other trail users: Trail runners
Special considerations: This is not as crowded a hike as Mount Beacon or many in the Hudson Highlands. If you're looking for a nature walk with some physical challenge, this is a good one.

MOHONK PRESERVE: BONTICOU CRAG

Start: Spring Farm parking area on Upper 27 Knolls Road in Mohonk Preserve
Elevation gain: 633 feet
Distance: 2.3-mile loop
Difficulty: Moderate to strenuous (You have a choice of routes.)
Hiking time: About 2 hours
Seasons: Spring through fall;
Schedule: Grounds open daily, sunrise to 1 hour after sunset
Fees and permits: Entry fee per person per day
Trail contact: Mohonk Preserve, PO Box 715, New Paltz, NY 12561; (845) 255-0919; mohonkpreserve.org

Dog-friendly: Dogs permitted on leash
Trail surface: Dirt and rock
Land status: Nonprofit nature preserve
Nearest town: New Paltz, New York
Other trail users: Mountain bikers, rock climbers, trail runners
Special considerations: This trail involves some tight squeezes and scrambling up rock faces; you have the option of skipping the most strenuous sections and taking an easier route. Some sections of the trail may be closed during peregrine falcon nesting season.

MINNEWASKA STATE PARK: VERKEERDERKILL FALLS TRAIL

Start: Parking area near the visitor center in Sam's Point Preserve
Elevation gain: 617 feet
Distance: 8.4-mile loop
Difficulty: Strenuous
Hiking time: About 5 hours
Seasons: Spring through fall
Schedule: Open daily, 9 a.m. to a time posted at the park entrance daily
Fees and permits: Entrance fee per vehicle per day in season from Memorial Day through Labor Day
Trail contact: Minnewaska State Park Preserve, 5281 Route 44-55, Kerhonkson, NY 12446; (845) 255-0752; nysparks.com/parks/127/details.aspx
Dog-friendly: Dogs permitted on leash
Trail surface: Crushed gravel carriage road to dirt path
Land status: New York state park preserve
Nearest town: Cragsmoor, New York
Other trail users: Hikers only
Special considerations: This trail was closed in 2017 because of a 2016 forest fire. Check with the park before planning a hike in this area. This waterfall is best viewed during a rainy season or after a rainstorm.

MINNEWASKA STATE PARK: RAINBOW FALLS TRAIL

Start: Lake Awosting parking area in Minnewaska State Park Preserve
Elevation gain: 430 feet
Distance: 5.4 miles out and back
Difficulty: Strenuous
Hiking time: About 4 hours
Seasons: Spring through fall
Schedule: Open daily, 9 a.m. to a time posted at the park entrance daily
Fees and permits: Entrance fee per vehicle per day in season from Memorial Day through Labor Day
Trail contact: Minnewaska State Park Preserve, 5281 Route 44-55, Kerhonkson, NY 12446; (845) 255-0752; nysparks.com/parks/127/details.aspx
Dog-friendly: Dogs permitted on leash
Trail surface: Crushed stone carriage road
Land status: New York state park preserve
Nearest town: Kerhonkson, New York
Other trail users: Hikers only
Special considerations: Parking in the park is limited to 500 cars and may fill up completely on summer weekends. Consider arriving early on summer and fall weekends or exploring this park on a weekday or in the off-season spring or fall. No swimming is allowed at the falls.

	BEST WATER-FALL HIKES	BEST SUMMIT HIKES	BEST URBAN/ SUBURBAN HIKES	BEST HIKES WITH SCRAM-BLING/ SQUEEZES	BEST HIKES WITH FABULOUS VIEWS
NEW YORK CITY AND THE PALISADES					
1 High Line			•		
2 Fort Lee Historic Park: Shore Trail–Long Path Loop			•		•
3 Croton Gorge Park	•				
4 Old Croton Aqueduct			•		
5 Teatown Lake Reservation			•		
6 Piermont Marsh and Pier			•		•
7 Anthony's Nose					•
PUTNAM AND ORANGE COUNTIES					
8 Little Stony Point		•			•
9 Hudson Highlands State Park Preserve: Cornish Estate–Undercliff Trail Loop				•	•
10 Breakneck Ridge				•	•
11 Clarence Fahnestock Memorial State Park: Three Lakes Trail					
12 Bear Mountain State Park: Appalachian Trail to the Summit		•			•
13 Storm King Mountain and Butter Hill		•		•	•
14 Harriman State Park: Pine Swamp Mountain		•			•
15 Constitution Marsh Audubon Center and Sanctuary					•
DUTCHESS COUNTY					
16 Tivoli Bays WMA					•
17 Mount Beacon Park		•			•
18 Thompson Pond					•
19 Dover Stone Church	•				

	BEST WATER-FALL HIKES	BEST SUMMIT HIKES	BEST URBAN/ SUBURBAN HIKES	BEST HIKES WITH SCRAM-BLING/ SQUEEZES	BEST HIKES WITH FABULOUS VIEWS
20 Locust Grove			●		
21 Walkway Over the Hudson State Historical Park			●		●
22 Peach Hill Park		●			●
23 Hyde Park Trail: Roosevelt and Vanderbilt National Historic Sites	●		●		
24 Top Cottage and Eleanor Roosevelt Estates			●		
25 Falling Waters Preserve	●		●		
26 Winnakee Nature Preserve					
27 Mount Egbert via the AT		●		●	
ULSTER COUNTY					
28 Minnewaska State Park Preserve, Minnewaska Lake Carriage Road					●
29 Minnewaska State Park Preserve, Sam's Point Area: Loop Road to the Ice Caves				●	
30 Black Creek Preserve					
31 Shaupeneak Ridge: Ridge Trail	●				●
32 Wallkill Valley Rail Trail					●
33 Upper Vernooy Kill Falls Trail	●				
COLUMBIA AND GREENE COUNTIES					
34 Taconic State Park: Copake Falls Mine Area and Bash Bish Falls	●				
35 Beebe Hill Fire Tower		●			●
36 North-South Lake Park: Catskill Escarpment Loop	●			●	●
37 Kaaterskill and Bastion Falls	●				
WESTERN CONNECTICUT					
38 The Audubon Center in Greenwich					
39 Lion's Head		●		●	●
40 Steep Rock Preserve: Steep Rock Loop					●

INDEX

Anthony's Nose, 49

Bear Mountain State Park: Appalachian Trail to the Summit, 80

Beebe Hill Fire Tower, 210

Black Creek Preserve, 181

Breakneck Ridge, 69

Clarence Fahnestock Memorial State Park: Three Lakes Trail, 74

Constitution Marsh Audubon Center and Sanctuary, 97

Croton Gorge Park, 27

Dover Stone Church, 120

Falling Waters Preserve, 153

Fort Lee Historic Park: Shore Trail–Long Path Loop, 20

Harriman State Park: Pine Swamp Mountain, 91

High Line Park, 15

Hudson Highlands State Preserve: Cornish Estate–Undercliff Trail Loop, 62

Hyde Park Trail: Roosevelt and Vanderbilt National Historic Sites, 140

Kaaterskill and Bastion Falls, 222

Lion's Head, 234

Little Stony Point, 56

Locust Grove, 125

Minnewaska State Park Preserve, Sam's Point Area: Loop Road to the Ice Caves, 176

Minnewaska State Park Preserve: Minnewaska Lake Carriage Road, 171

Mount Beacon Park, 109

Mount Egbert via the Appalachian Trail, 164

North-South Lake Park: Catskill Escarpment Loop, 216

Old Croton Aqueduct Trail: Scarborough to Sleepy Hollow, 33

Peach Hill Park, 135

Piermont Marsh and Pier, 44

Shaupeneak Ridge: Ridge Trail, 187

Steep Rock Preserve: Steep Rock Loop, 239

Storm King Mountain and Butter Hill, 85

Taconic State Park: Copake Falls Mine Area and Bash Bish Falls, 205

Teatown Lake Reservation, 39

The Audubon Center in Greenwich, 228

Thompson Pond, 114

Tivoli Bays Wildlife Management Area, 104

Top Cottage and Eleanor Roosevelt Estate, 148

Upper Vernooy Kill Falls Trail, 198

Walkway Over the Hudson State Historic Park and Loop Trail, 130

Wallkill Valley Rail Trail: New Paltz to Rosendale, 192

Winnakee Nature Preserve, 159

ABOUT THE AUTHOR AND PHOTOGRAPHER

Wife-and-husband team Randi and Nic Minetor are delighted to return to the Hudson River Valley for Nic's third and Randi's fifth book on this region. They have collaborated on twenty-five books for FalconGuides, Lyons Press, and Globe Pequot about hiking, birding, exploring historic cities, and America's national parks. Their popular books on outdoor activities in New York State include *Hiking Waterfalls in New York*, *Hiking Through History New York*, and five *Best Easy Day Hikes* guides: Rochester, Buffalo, Syracuse, Albany, and the Hudson River Valley. In addition, they worked together on eight Quick Reference Guides to the native birds, trees, and wildflowers of New York City, New York State, and the Middle Atlantic states. Randi is also the author of *Day Trips: Hudson River Valley*, and the Minetors worked together on *Backyard Birding: A Guide to Attracting and Identifying Birds*, *Scenic Routes and Byways New York*, and *The New England Bird Lover's Garden*.

When not on the trail, Randi writes for magazines in the theatre technology, municipal water distribution, and medical trades, as well as for a number of reference publishers. Nic is the resident lighting designer for several theatre and opera companies in upstate New York, and for the PBS series "Second Opinion." The Minetors live in Rochester, NY.